General Elzbieta Zawacka

Polish secret agent during World War Two, aliases Elizabeth Kubitza, Elizabeth von Brauneg, Mme. Elise Rivière, Zofia Zajkowska, Elizabeth Watson and code-names Zelma, Zo and Sulica

Bernard O'Connor

Acknowledgements

I need to acknowledge Sue Ryder, whose autobiography contained Elzbieta's wartime memoirs and the National Archives in Kew for providing access to Elzbieta's personnel file. I need to thank Steven Kippax, the SOE historian, who very kindly provided a copy of this file and all his efforts in copying and disseminating SOE documents. Fred Judge helped resolve many of the SOE code-words. Heide Pirwitz and Eugenia Marech of the Polish Underground Movement Study Trust were particularly helpful and Marta Kurkowska-Budzan kindly provided Anna Muller's academic paper.

This work would not have been possible without other historians, past and present, undertaking their own research, notably Freddy Clark, Ewa and Bogumil Liszewskich, Eugenia Maresch, Katarzyna Minczykowska. Anna Muller, David Oliver, Sue Ryder, Ian Valentine and Jonathan Walker.

The following websites were particularly useful, not only for their information about Elzbieta, her life and times, but also for their illustrations: army.cz, biega.com, collections.yadvashem.org/ cowtonruniu.pl, culture24.org, delcampe.net, derelictplace.co.uk, dsh.waw.pl, drieje.pl, englishheritage.org, hoteletatsunisopera.com, Imperial War Museum, i.ytimg.com, kohr.kujawsko-pomorskie.pl, niepoprawn.pl, nieziomni.com, nightingalemansion.org, nowahistoria.interia.pl, panoramio.com, personalpages. manchester.ac.uk, rp.pl, shipsnostalgia.com, special forcesroh.com, terresdescrains.com, tripadvisor.com, um.torun.pl, Wikipedia, Wikimedia, ww2incolour.com and wyorcza.pl.

Bernard O'Connor 2014
www.bernardoconnor.org.uk

Whilst researching the women secret agents who were infiltrated into occupied Europe during World War Two, I read in David Oliver's *Airborne Espionage* that Elzbieta Zawacka was the first woman agent sent into Poland on 9 September 1943. She was parachuted from Squadron Leader Krol's plane with Wireless Operator Klosowski at the controls. (Oliver, D. (2005), *Airborne Espionage: International Special Duties Operations in the World Wars,* The History Press, Stroud, p.112) ,

The airfield was RAF Tempsford, about half way between Cambridge and Bedford and about fifty miles north of London. It was the base of 138 and 161 Special Duties Squadrons, who flew without lights during the nights on either side of the full moon to supply the resistance movements across Western and Eastern Europe, parachute arms, ammunition, supplies and specially-trained agents behind enemy lines and to land agents and pick up passengers to be returned to Britain. (O'Connor, B. (2013), *Churchill's Angels,* Amberley Press)

Freddy Clark, one of the Special Duty Squadron pilots, reported in his *Agents by Moonlight*, that on the night of 9/10th September 1943, the Polish C Flight of 138 Squadron, flew six missions to Poland. Squadron Leader Krol and his Polish crew flew a converted Handley Halifax bomber on a mission, code-named NEON 4, and dropped three agents, one package and six containers of stores. Despite being attacked and hit by a Messerschmitt 110, Krol got back safely to Tempsford. Two of the other missions to Poland were aborted and the three others dropped six containers and six packages. Clark did not give the agents' names. (Clark, F. (1999), *Agents by Moonlight*, Tempus, p.190)

Research on various websites revealed that Elzbieta was born on 19 March 1909 in Torun, about 260 km. northwest of Warsaw in Prussia, what was then the German part of partitioned Poland. Her father, Wladyslaw, was an official at the Court of Justice in Torun and her mother, Marianna, looked after her and the other seven children, Marianne, John, Eric, Egon, Adelaide, Alfonso and Klara. They were brought up Roman Catholic with a strong Polish patriotic tradition but, as her mother wanted them all to be educated; they had to speak German for fear of her father losing his job and the family being persecuted. She only started learning Polish when she was nine, following Poland gaining independence in 1918.

After finishing her education at the Girls Secondary School of Humanities, she graduated in mathematics from Adam Mickiewicz University in Poznan. Unbeknown to her, one of her professors, Professor Krygowski, also taught the cryptologists, Marian Rejewski, Jerzy Rozycki and Henryk Zygalski, who went on to work for the Polish Cipher bureau in Warsaw and break the German Enigma code in 1933.

During the 1920s and 30s she worked in the Post Office, as a tutor and, from 1936, as a teacher in a secondary school in the Tarnów Mountains. She was also a Scout instructor which helped keep her fit and provided valuable experience in outdoor survival skills. In 1937 she qualified as an instructor for the PWK, an organisation responsible for training women for military service, and was responsible for nineteen districts in Silesia. The introduction of conscription on 4 September 1938 provided the opportunity for women to fight, but only in an auxiliary role, something Elzbieta was determined to change. (http://facet.wp.pl/ kat,1034179,wid,14344761,wiadom osc. html? ticaid=112c70; http://www.zawacka.pl/monodram. ht ml; http://nowahistoria.interia.pl/polska-walczaca/news-elz bieta-zawacka-jedyna-kobieta-wsrod-cichociemnych,nId,1 059279; Maresch, E. *"Zo"* – *General Elzbieta Zawacka*, Rocznkarchwalno-Historycznycaw; Ryder, S. (1986), *Child of my Love*, Collins Harvill, pp.89, 117)

In a post-war interview with Anna Muller, Elzbieta

admitted that, aware of the coming war, her two aims were to defend Poland and to ensure women soldiers had the same rights as the men.

When I went to my first PWK camp, my ordinary life ended and there was only PWK in my life. I worked and studied. I was a teacher and even liked it. But first of all, I was the instructor of PWK. Then 1939 came. The work for PWK was the most important. You don't know this feeling when the motherland is in danger. I was a soldier. We knew that a war is coming and we knew that we had to prepare women as part of a regular army. I have been growing with the thought of war since December of 1930, since I was part of PWK. (Muller, A. *Oral History; The Challenges of Dialogue*, Edited by Marta Kurkowska-Budzan and Krysztof Zamorski, John Benjamins Publishing Company, (2009), pp.118-9)

When Germany invaded Poland on 1 September 1939, Elzbieta was 30 and recalled her father crying when German troops marched into Torun. She was mobilised and served as a commandant in the Przyspos Obienie Wojskowe Kobiet (PWK), the Polish Women's Military Training Organisation in Katowice, Silesia, and in September took 15 women instructors to organise anti-aircraft and anti-tank defences around Lwow (Lviv), a city in what is now Western Ukraine, which was under siege by the Germans. When the Soviet Red Army invaded Eastern Poland on 17 October, the Germans retreated and she recalled thinking at a meeting of Polish officers

Lviv is giving up. What are you choosing? We had to choose something. The choices are – Russian captivity, escape to civilian life, or escape through Hungary and France. You have to decide…the end…

there were so many suicides, so many...because they did not know what to do. What is going to happen to us? What to choose? What is the right choice? Can I handle it? (Ibid.p.119)

She decided to remain in the military, went to Warsaw and when she heard the message 'White dress is ready', knew that she had been accepted into the Polish Anti-Nazi resistance, the Polish underground army. In October she was sworn into the Służba Zwycięstwu Polski (Polish Victory Service, the first Polish resistance movement in World War Two. This was later transformed into the *Związek Walki Zbrojnej* (ZWZ), Association of Military Struggle, and in 1940, code-named 'Zelma', she was appointed head of communications in ZWZ's headquarters.

At the end of 1940, she worked as a courier for 'Zagroda', the Department of Foreign Communications, which was code-named 'Circus'. It was responsible for maintaining contact between the Polish Resistance groups in other European countries as well as the government-in-exile in London. When she went to Denmark, she used the alias Elizabeth von Brauneg. According to the Wikipedia website, she also visited Sweden but documentation to confirm it has come to light.

According to Muller, Elzbieta became a legendary figure in the Home Army organising the western routes out of Poland. She also taught in the secret teaching organisation (TON) at Zymichowskiej school in Warsaw and, using the code-names of 'Zo' and 'Sulica', undertook over a hundred missions using false identity papers to carry money, messages and reports to and from Polish agents in occupied Western Europe as well as intelligence that had to be transmitted to London. When she was back in Warsaw, she taught others the skills she had acquired so that they could act as couriers. (Ibid, pp.119-20; Minczykowska, K. *Elizabeth Zawacka, "Zelma", "Sulica", "Zo"* (series: Library

Foundation Archive Pomeranian AK', t L), Torun 2008, ed. Foundation 'Archives and Museum Pomeranian AK' in Torun; Maresch, op.cit.)

After the war, Elzbieta gave Baroness Ryder of Warsaw a long and detailed account of her wartime activities. As shall be seen, Ryder played a prominent role with Polish agents in England, engaged in numerous charitable ventures in Poland and set up the Sue Ryder care homes. She included Elzbieta's memoirs in her autobiography, *Child of My Love.*

As a courier between 1941- 42 I often had to travel to Berlin, but I could not risk going by the most direct way from Warsaw via Poznan as the Gestapo kept all the main trains, especially the international ones, under close observation. I was obliged therefore to use an alternative route via Torun or via Silesia in the south of Poland. The routes also depended on whether I had contacted a person in the Resistance where I could leave or collect messages.

Once in May 1942 while travelling from Berlin to a contact point in Silesia where I had hoped to spend the night, I was carrying rather a large and heavy suitcase – this had a false compartment which was full of dollars. In this suitcase I also carried some clothing and whatever else I could pack in to disguise the weight of the money. My route lay through a place called Sosnowiec. There I should have found my sister [20-year-old Klara] and a colleague who I knew would give me a bed for the night. Because I had the documents of a Reich-German, who therefore was not Polish, I could travel after the hours of curfew. It was the 25th May 1942 when I arrived at my sister's door and knocked, but nobody answered. I then went to a neighbour's house and knocked; she opened the door and went absolutely white with shock on seeing me.

She wanted to close the door on me, but I put my foot in and asked why she was behaving in this way and what had happened to my sister Klara. She said "The Gestapo are here and they have arrested both your sister and her colleague, Nina."

At that time they arrested several cells of people in the Resistance in Silesia and I think there had been a general round-up, but I had not heard of it. I had come from Berlin and found myself in a situation where the Gestapo were on the look-out for any suspicious people, but fortunately the arrests had taken place four days earlier. Nevertheless, they were still watching the house, but by pure chance they had just left to have a meal before I arrived. It was really a miracle as my sister was already being interrogated by the Gestapo. I took the suitcase very quickly and went as calmly as I could to another colleague, Stacha. (Later she was arrested and beheaded in Katowice at the end of July 1942.) I was lucky to find that Stacha was still free; she belonged to a different cell and I was able to stay there until 3 a.m., and she told me what was happening but, of course, I still had the suitcase with me. I also realised that it was my duty to inform as many people as I could about what was happening, no next day I took the suitcase to the station and deposited it in the left luggage department and received a receipt for it.

From the station I went into one of the streets; it was not the main street, but nevertheless quite a busy one, and I managed to meet one or two of our people and I said to them very quickly "Get away from here", but, unfortunately, I made the mistake of remaining there too long. An agent had noticed me and I knew that I was being observed and followed. I boarded a tram still in Sosnowiec, but two Gestapo men in plain clothes got on as well. The tram went to Katowice. I got off there and tried various means to lose them but could not, so I had to proceed to Krakow.

On the way, there was a frontier post at Trzebinia. I was absolutely soaked with perspiration from fear and I thought that when we were checked they would see my papers. The Gestapo presumably told the frontier control people that they were watching me. Of course, they carried with them blacklists in which perhaps one of my names appeared. I was amazed not to have been arrested. When I arrived at Krakow I was absolutely exhausted. I was trying all the time to disguise myself completely in whatever way I could to keep ahead of them, but there was absolutely no other way but to go to a colleague and say to her, "Look, help me, try and see if they are still there." My colleague, Celina Zawadzinska (later arrested and sent to Ravensbrück), looked out and saw one of the Gestapo waiting for me so I had to leave her. I asked her to follow this Gestapo member at a safe distance herself to see what happened to me and then to disappear before curfew. Furthermore, the Gestapo kept changing. I arrived late in the evening at Krakow station, by which time it was dark. I waited a long time. At 11 p.m. there was an express train to Warsaw and I entered a compartment reserved for Germans only. Of course, I had a thousand thoughts in my head but, before boarding the train, I managed to observe on the platform a colleague from Warsaw. She kept walking up and down. I found a tiny piece of paper and wrote on it, "One has broken down under torture and is therefore likely to give away the names of other people. I am under observation and being followed by the Gestapo." I was able to get near to her and simply handed her this crumpled piece of paper. She was an extremely experienced member of the Resistance and she turned away as though she did not know me at all; at the same time, of course, I gave her to understand that if I was taken she, in turn, should warn the others. At that moment I felt that at last I could breathe. I later discovered that the reason why the person had given some people away was that the Gestapo had put her on an electric bed and after this and other methods of torture she broke down.

I was still frightened and wanted to jump from the express train. I kept wondering whether to try and get out before daylight, but I realised the dangers, not only from the drop but also of falling onto the track which might have killed me, and I did not want to die. On the other hand, I knew that I had to get out of that train because if I remained on it and arrived in Warsaw I would be arrested. Also, I did not carry with me a poison tablet. As the train approached the town of Zyrardow (48 kilometres from Warsaw) there was a curve on the line and the train started to slow down a bit. It was about 4 a.m. I knew the moment had arrived when I simply had to get out. I left the compartment as though to go to the toilet and walked along the corridor. I realised, of course, that I was still under observation, but I had left my small insignificant packet in the compartment before going to the toilet. The third carriage was the last; and the last carriage always had a rear window. I went to the last door and saw a Polish railway official; he held the door and I sprang out. When one is in such a dangerous situation one has odd thoughts and as I jumped I remembered that I had heard in America and other countries tramps and people who were homeless often jumped up in the air before going down. However, I fell on knees and arms, which started to bleed, and I rolled over into a ditch. I thought that the Gestapo would stop the train and I hoped that they would not have bloodhounds.

With blistered hands and painful legs I started to make haste towards the woods. I remember two men looking at me curiously, as if I had been mad! I ran further and saw a woman with a shawl over her head who looked like a factory worker. I took off my jacket and a gold ring and gave them to her and she in exchange hurriedly gave me her things and some bread she was carrying which I needed badly as I was so hungry. I threw away my shoes and washed the blood off my legs, feet and arms and tried to disguise myself as a simple girl from the country. The sun had risen, but I continued to walk for miles keeping well away from the railway line and I felt tired. Finally, I came to a railway station and I asked a Pole, "Please give me some money, I must go to Warsaw." The Pole immediately gave me the money I needed and I caught the next train to Warsaw. (During the Occupation we were all brothers and sisters regardless of being strangers.)

I believed that the Gestapo had lost sight of me so I quickly went to a contact point where my friend, Wanda, gave me a coat and I felt calm and relieved to be with her.

My poor sister Klara – by profession a lawyer – was by now in prison in Sosnowiec together with many of her fellow "workers". She survived difficult interrogations as she knew the German language fluently and was able to give shrewd replies to their continual questions. Despite all these, she maintained she could not give them any information. Klara spent six months in that prison. My other sister, Dela, sent her food parcels but a large proportion of these was stolen and eaten by the SS warders.

Meanwhile, I was still thinking about the suitcase which I had left behind. I had managed to leave the receipt for this with a pharmacist in Katowice. I reported this to the cell in which I worked in the Resistance and a courier named Tadeusz, together with another member of the Resistance, were sent with haste from Warsaw to fetch it. From Krakow, Tadeusz was obliged to cross the frontier to Katowice in Silesia. As he had left in a hurry he did not have the right documents, and on reaching the frontier he secretly paid a guide to help him cross the border illegally.

When Tadeusz reached the pharmacy it was unfortunately closed. He lost valuable time in searching for the pharmacist. This put him in greater danger and when he realised that his contact was nervous he did not feel it was fair to stay the night there and he therefore resorted to hiding in a haystack in a nearby village. By burying himself in the hay he felt all the more dishevelled.

Eventually he succeeded in obtaining the receipt and went to the left luggage office at the railway station in Katowice. As he approached he noticed a German standing nearby who seemed to be taking a great interest in him. At the moment of handing over the receipt to the German clerk, he had the presence of mind to engage them in conversation (only the German language was allowed to be spoken and he knew it fluently). He also knew that some Germans could be bribed and he therefore offered both men a cigar. This enabled him to get out of the station with the suitcase and walk away as naturally as possible.

Thanks to his cool courage, the contents of the suitcase, which were invaluable for the work, were saved. All this meant however that I could no longer travel to Berlin as I was now on the wanted list by the Gestapo under my real name of Elizabeth Zawacka, born 19th March 1909 in Torun. So, I had to change my whole appearance. I dyed my hair red and took to wearing a very large hat. I received a new name, forged identity card and waited for a new mission.

I was extremely lucky to be given a seemingly improbable order to prepare myself for a long journey. I was told [by General Stefan Grot Kowecki of the Home

Army, (Maresch, op.cit, p.10] to cross almost the whole of Europe – several thousand kilometres – and reach [General Wladyslaw Sikorski] the General Staff of the Polish forces in London. I had to take messages and act as an Emissary of the Home Army Headquarters to discuss (1) the different routes taken by couriers, and (2) as a pre-war instructor of the Women's Military Training Service, I was to report the different problems connected with the organisation of the Polish Military Women's Service in our Secret Army.

A few of my colleagues said this mission would be a reward for the difficulties I had experienced beforehand.

The preparation took a long time. It was difficult to procure fool-proof forged documents so that the route could be relatively safe. I had to memorise all the details of the complicated network of our liaison stations spread all over Europe. I also had to learn quite a lot of different things, including some knowledge of the English language. I studied the existing routes and read for weeks different decoded secret documents hitherto hidden in archives.

On 17 December 1942 I set out by train from Warsaw to Paris via Berlin and Strasbourg. My new name was Elizabeth Kubitza and I was officially employed as a clerk to a petroleum firm which had branches in both Warsaw and Paris. (I was bilingual in German and Polish.)

I reached Paris safely after feeling frightened whilst crossing two frontiers, the first near Kutno between G.G. (General Government) [the German term for Poland] and the Reich, the second one near Strasbourg, Germany/France. The journey from Warsaw to Paris lasted about 48 hours.

In Paris there was a liaison group base/cell from Zagroda (a division of the Home Army in Poland) under the code name Janka which operated with Ceux de la Liberation Vengeance, part of the French Gaullist organisation and under the control of Colonel Médéric.

Janka was trying to prepare a route for me to the unoccupied part of France and then on to Spain. The way was via Vichy and Perpignan in the East Pyrenees, to Figueras in Spain, and then to the British Consulate in Barcelona. My pseudonym in France was now Mme. Elise Rivière from Alsace. As my mission was so vital and I carried such important messages, I had received an order to be certain of the security of the route, but this route was a new one and had not been tested before by any other courier.

Amongst the people in the French Resistance who were helping us was an engine driver. He drove a special train which sometimes carried Laval [Head of the French Vichy government]. The train travelled regularly from the Gare d'Orléans Station in Paris to Vichy. It crossed the dangerous border between Occupied and Unoccupied France. This engine driver took me and another courier called Pankrac. We had to climb the narrow opening into the tender attached to the locomotive which carried water. This was located behind the engine. We had to lie on hard wooden boards over the splashing water in the tender. We lay on these boards from the evening until early the next morning waiting to start. It was mid-December 1942. At 3 a.m. the engine driver, who was clearly upset, came and called to us in the tender, "You must get out because another courier, Wilski, who left on the route you intend to follow is already in the hands of the Gestapo near Narbonne." He (the engine driver) had received a very urgent message from the Pyrenees to give us the warning.

It was still very dark and I remember that I had turned my coat inside out in order to prevent it looking too dirty. We got out and the French driver led us very cautiously through the station to his own flat. There were many Germans on patrol in different parts of the station.

Pankrac went to a different flat. He knew Paris better than I did and had more contact points. He had also been a student there before the War. (He was later sent to Spain. There he was arrested and taken to the concentration camp in Miranda, from which he was later released. Then he joined General Sikorski at Gibraltar and boarded the same ill-fated aircraft there. In Pankrac's last notes which were found later he had written, "I reached the summit of my life when I reported to General Sikorski.")

I remained with the engine driver's family for about two days.

The organiser of routes for Zagroda in France, called Bradl (Kazimierz Leski), suggested to me that I should try another route. We went to Bordeaux and from there to Bayonne. We had two possibilities there. The first was to travel via St Jean de Luz to find a boat which could take me to the Spanish side, to Irun in the Basque country and from there, with luck, to Pamplona. Unfortunately, we could not find a guide so we went to Pau where it was proposed that I should travel in a truck amongst cattle, but this did not seem a sensible or realistic proposition, so I returned to Paris.

The other idea was to receive guidance and help from Andrzej Lipkowski. He had a cousin who was manager of a bank in Paris and his family had lived in France for many years. He also knew Colonel Médéric. He told me that there might even be a remote possibility of being picked up by a Lysander aircraft (a light, single engine reconnaissance aircraft with a very short take-off and landing capability) which I though sounded unbelievable. I had not heard about these pickups before and it seemed a fantastic idea.

I waited in Paris some days over Christmas in order to satisfy myself that I had tried everything. Then I resumed my *other* identity, of Elizabeth Kubitza, and crossed the whole of Germany back to Warsaw. During the two days I was returning from Paris to Warsaw I had no more food coupons and only managed to find a celery salad in Berlin. As always, I was frightened but at any rate I reached my beloved capital and explained the situation to my commanding officer, Marcysia.

As I was considered to be an experienced courier who had travelled to many different parts of Europe, I was given my head to decide upon which route I should follow from Warsaw the *second* time. Meantime, I had other work to do for about four weeks which a new and equally essential assignment had been prepared for me to take on. This comprised a few hundred pages of ciphered microfilmed typescript and drawings hidden in a key and a cigarette lighter.

So, on the 17th February 1943, I started out again and travelled as Elizabeth Kubitza.

There, in Paris, for the *second* time I reported again to the German Ortskommandantur in order to exchange my food coupons from Warsaw and obtain my original French ones which I had left with them – both lots were forged. I also had to obtain a hotel billet. The Germans would not issue the coupons immediately as they had on the *first* journey, and they told me to stay overnight at the Hotel Cadet near the Metro and to return the following day to collect them. I did not know why they had said this. I was carrying the secret post and felt terrified during the hours of darkness that the Gestapo might arrest me, so I walked up and down the hotel room wondering what on earth to do. I had a sleepless night.

The next morning I returned to the German office

where, to my amazement, I heard them saying to one another, "Look at these food coupons...they are the right ones and the others (meaning the legal ones) should look like these!" Such was my relief that I went to a coffee shop and treated myself to some coffee, some ham and a glass of wine.

While in Paris I followed a short course in Spanish at the Paris Berlitz School. I then reverted to my French identity of Elise Rivière.

Again, on my second attempt to reach London, the same engine driver hid me in the tender in Laval's train, but this time with no less than eight young Frenchmen who were attempting to escape to join the Free French forces. I was not accompanied by another Polish courier. We all had to lie on the boards over the water. I was carrying my messages again in a lighter and a key.

I cannot remember the time of night we crossed the border between the two zones, but I arrived in Vichy early in the morning. I was able to look at the park. Then we boarded different trains for Toulouse. I had the opportunity of seeing the most beautiful small medieval town of Carcassonne. We slept on the station at Toulouse and felt very stiff and tired, but I was in the company of young and optimistic Frenchmen. Then we continued our journey to a village close to Tarascon, near the French frontier. On the way we had numerous checks and had to go through control points manned by French gendarmes under the direction of the German authority. The young Frenchmen were naturally very anxious, but fortunately we reached our destination.

Along the frontier in the different mountain villages quite a number of Spaniards were living amongst the French people. They had escaped from Franco's regime and a few of them were either smugglers or guides. The young Frenchmen in whose company I was, found a young man called Paco Bonne, a young Catalonian, who was to be our first guide, and I gave him some money. I was the only person in the group who had enough money, because in Warsaw I had been given two gold sovereigns and a number of dollars. I asked him whether he could somehow manage to find a compass for me, or even a map of the Pyrenees, but neither could be found.

I wore a blue coat and bound my feet with woollen strips, like gaiters, to protect them as well as possible from the elements. Paco asked us to meet him at a small country inn in a village not far from Tarascon at 8 p.m. that evening. There we waited in a narrow, dimly-lit corridor from which a door led into the main room of the restaurant. Suddenly, to our horror, instead of Paco, two Germans entered. They were from the Special Mountain Police and wore the Edelweiss insignia on their caps. While one went to the telephone, the second started to question each of us about the identity cards we carried. It would have been very difficult indeed to explain what an Alsatian woman, who spoke only moderate French, was doing there. I succeeded in moving to the end of the row and hid behind a cupboard where I managed to remove my coat. The following moments were terrible and my legs felt like jelly.

The young Frenchmen were very naïve as conspirators and had great difficulty in answering the Germans' questions. As they reached the third or fourth person I slipped through a second smaller door into the restaurant and snatched an apron from an astonished waitress. I noticed that there was a radio playing and quickly turned up the volume. I had also noticed that there was a simple wooden staircase and as I mounted this I felt a hand on my arm and realised it was Paco.

He had been waiting upstairs and, seeing the Germans, he realised what was happening. Naturally, he was also frightened. He grabbed me by the arm and took me through a little door which led directly out onto the mountainside. I hid as best I could behind a bush and waited. Later I heard the roar of an engine. My unhappy companions were being taken away by the Germans but, by a miracle, it seemed I had been saved. It was exceedingly cold, especially as I was rather high up in the mountains and it was towards the end of February. Unexpectedly, I felt someone put a warm jacket round me. It was Gilbert, who became a new friend of mine. I was taken to a room where there were some Spaniards and remained there for two or three days.

I kept on asking, "Please give me a map, for I want to go on alone," but understandably they had no map.

I still had a little money on me so I could try to cross the mountains again. Meanwhile Paco Bonne organised a fairly large group of smugglers which included his uncle. This was the *second* attempt and in this group two Jews were included who had succeeded in escaping from Vienna to the Pyrenees. One was tall, the other short, and both were very poor and thin. There was a full moon and it was bitterly cold. The place from which we were leaving had ruins of historical Roman baths, and we set off with Paco Bonne and his uncle. We started to climb and came upon a stream which was absolutely frozen. As one or two in the company started to cross it, the ice cracked. There was a noise and suddenly we heard a shot ring out – fired by the Germans – and we hid behind some marble columns. Crouching down we wondered what would happen next. The others had disappeared. Later, one of the Spaniards, a guide, took me by the arm and led me to a mountain hut. Perhaps this man knew that I had a little money, but I was fast running out of this and only three one-dollar notes remained stitched in my clothing.

When I met Paco Bonne again I had been obliged to admit that I had little or no money, but to strengthen my case I felt it was necessary to tell him that I worked for the Intelligence Service, "If you get me over this frontier," I said, "I cannot pay you, but I will recommend you to the Consul as a good guide." He was not very happy with this, but at last I convinced him that this was my *third* attempt. Again, I had to wait two to three days because Paco Bonne had to choose the right night. It was essential to know the movements of the frontier guards and at what time the Germans changed their shifts etc., so we re-grouped with the two Jews still in the party.

In addition to Bonne, there was the young Frenchman called Gilbert, whom I mentioned earlier. He came from the Pas de Calais, northern France. I got to know him quite quickly. He was a woodcutter and in this way he was able to make money and pay a guide, for his aim was to reach North Africa and join the Free French forces.

About twenty of us started to climb the mountains. The going was extremely rough, and after some hours a very severe blizzard descended on us. The guide lost his way. We continued to battle on in this freezing cold with the added hazard of the blizzard. Nevertheless, we somehow managed to keep going at a reasonable pace but the weakest, including the two unfortunate Jews, fell back. One of them simply said he could not go on. I had finished my small ration of chocolate and only had a little sugar left, so I gave him this and we were obliged to leave them.

After walking for hours we found a rough stone mountain hut. The route had proved extremely difficult because it was full of stones which we continually stumbled over in the blizzard. I remember the snow came up to my waist and Bonne had to try and clear a way. Those who remained felt exhausted. The mountain hut was used during the summer for sheep, and we had to clear out the snow which had blown inside. We then lay down and slept for three to four hours. The worst aspect (apart from the weather) was the fact that the guide had completely lost his way. He had no means of knowing where we were. My lips were swollen, chapped and bleeding, and the only fluid I had taken was from licking snow. I had no food left. We continued walking for about twenty hours when suddenly we came upon a heap of snow where I saw a frozen arm sticking out: it was one of the Jews we had left behind. He had fallen into the snow and frozen to death.

Later I realised that the others had deserted us and I was alone with Paco Bonne and Gilbert. Paco Bonne led, I was in the middle and Gilbert helped to push me. Bonne confidently said to us, "We shall arrive quite soon at the frontier." As we went on we came to the cliffs and we paused to gather our breath and strength. I listened to the stillness and I heard German voices. Looking down on the snow I saw an empty packet of German cigarettes. We were terrified. As we came to realise our position we started to run down the mountain as fast as we could and reached a dried up river bed full of stones. Some of these stones were so sharp that it was a miracle we did not break our bones.

At last the weather improved, and after about an hour Paco Bonne realised where we were. In fact, we were far too near a hut used by German frontier patrols. Paco knew that at certain times the frontier shifts changed, but we continued to be exceedingly concerned and wondered whether the guards were alone or accompanied by dogs. We hid in a deep ditch.

The snow covered us and the Germans passed by, fortunately without dogs. We resumed walking and after some hours we came to another mountain hut where an acquaintance of Paco Bonne's was waiting. He led us up into the loft and I slept for 24 hours. When they woke me they brought some food. I had recovered my strength and returned to the same village. Then we had to start thinking how we were to make a *fourth* attempt. Paco Bonne either could not or would not undertake the journey, and so his uncle agreed to do so. He did not appear to be particularly friendly. Two other Frenchmen had joined Gilbert and me, so there were five of us this time.

We had to continue to plod through the night in order not to be seen by the German frontier guards. This time, too, the guide led us through some very difficult parts of the mountain and about two or three o'clock in the morning, when it was coldest, I simply could not continue and lay down in the snow – I was unable to go on. The guide was pretty severe. He roused me by kicking me and then sprayed some wine into my mouth from his flask which gave me strength. I got up and continued walking. Gradually the dawn broke and I saw the most beautiful sight in my life, an alpine glow.

As the sun rose it threw its rays upon the high peaks. Other parts of the mountains were still dark and it seemed that the higher peaks were bathed in a kind of glorious pink and then in red gold, like fire. This was an absolutely marvellous scene and somehow made me forget my tiredness. I also saw mountain goat and an eagle. We still had several hours of walking ahead. Then from afar we saw the frontier guards. The guide had binoculars and he ordered us to drop down on the ground and wait until the guards went away. It became exceedingly hot with the sun shining on the snow, and at about ten or eleven o'clock the guide suddenly announced, "Ahead of this next high peak lies Spain and you must now continue alone." The two Frenchmen went on ahead as they were quicker, and Gilbert and I walked more slowly behind. It was very hard to climb and after reaching the top of the mountain we first walked down but then decided to sit and slide gently down part of the other side. After that we ran.

We thought we had at last reached Spain. We were on the south side of the Pyrenees and it was warm in spite of there being a lot of snow. As we descended we reached a little stream and I sat on a big flat stone covered with snow and said to Gilbert, "Go and look, there are some houses over there." When he came back he said with some surprise, "Yes, there is a village, but it is in *Andorra* and not Spain!" As we approached the village we were naturally still nervous.

In Andorra there was a nest of smugglers. Gilbert took me to an inn and the woman there brought me a plate of fried potatoes and oranges. I was greatly relieved to be able to go to bed as I felt so terribly tired. I slept until the evening. Gilbert, who was between 20 and 25 years of age, was intelligent and energetic and discovered an Englishman in the village, a Mr Robert, who I thought worked for British Intelligence. Gilbert already knew this although we were not able to converse with Mr Robert easily as my knowledge of English was limited. In the evening Mr Robert came to see me again and I said to him, "I am a courier from Poland and I have a password to convey to the British Consul in Barcelona." He believed me and said I should sleep in the same inn.

The next morning he arrived in a black car in the village street and from this village of Old Andorra we drove to the capital, Santa Julia. On the way we passed the two astonished Frenchmen who had left us earlier. I was in rags and completely filthy. My shoes were in tatters. Mr Robert handed me over to another person who took me to a good hotel where I remained until the evening. Meanwhile they had bought me some local shoes made from thick plaited string called espadrilles. In the evening another guide turned up. He had been a District Officer and because he had fought against Franco knew that if caught he would be hanged.

We proceeded on foot towards the Andorra/Spanish frontier. It took us two to three hours. As we made our way down the mountain we were perpetually on the lookout for frontier guards and the situation continued to be dangerous. It was not quite so cold but snow was still thick on the ground. Gilbert kept reminding me that I was not keeping up the pace and he found me heavy to push. We faced yet another mountain to cross and the going was hard. Finally, we reached a primitive stone hut where we lit a fire and in a very simple pot cooked some scrambled eggs. There were no lights but only a holder fixed to the wall in which wood shavings topped with tar were burnt to give light. Afterwards I was taken up to the hay loft where I slept soundly. I remember wearing a light -coloured scarf over my head to stop the hay getting into my hair.

The guide woke us early the next morning. There were three of us. We emerged from the hut and started the descent. It was a bit foggy. We thought, mistakenly, that we were relatively safe and far from the enemy and foolishly spoke too loudly. Apart from this my light scarf was conspicuous. Suddenly, the guide who carried my small bag started to run. He had very long legs and got away from us very quickly. At the same time Gilbert also left me. They had seen two guards! Naturally I also started to run as fast as I could because they were shooting and fortunately I reached a tall rock with bushes which I climbed and knelt down covering my face and hands as I had been trained to do. I knew I could not go any further as I would have been in sight of the guards who continued to fire; as it was the bullets went over my head and to either side of me.

Meanwhile, I quickly removed my headscarf. By this time the guards were standing at the foot of the cliff and were able to see Gilbert and the guide running far away in the distance and they continued to shoot at them but failed to hit them. The guards stood awhile, talked a bit and then, to my relief, walked away. I sat in a crouched position a long time and wondered what on earth to do next as I was alone without a map and practically no money. I knew only a few words of Spanish. It was still early in the morning and pretty cold and I began inadvertently to sneeze. Gilbert heard this noise and so was able to find me. I think, too, he returned because I was on his conscience.

The three dollars and the vital information and reports remained stitched inside my clothing. We continued to walk in the mountains searching for a village. We found a stream, but this did not run in the right direction. Then, in the afternoon, we saw from afar and below a village and an orchard of almond trees in blossom – a beautiful sight. The village appeared to be deserted as the workers were busy somewhere. We went into the first empty building – a small house – and climbed a ladder in order to hide. We did not know what to expect so we remained under the roof and waited. Later an old man appeared. I gave him my last three dollars and he handed me some cold cooked beans. He left to go into the village. We did not know if he would denounce us or what he would do. Hours later, in the evening, he returned with a very nice teacher and a donkey and the teacher brought us to his simple classroom. He also wanted me to listen to the BBC and give him news. We were unable to sleep in the classroom and he took us to his two frugal civilised hotel where I met Czechs who had also escaped. Whilst waiting again I looked briefly round Madrid and then continued on my route to Gibraltar.

The frontier crossing from Spain to Gibraltar was naturally very well guarded because the British authorities suspected Germans and their agents of gathering any information they could about convoys, etc., and everybody was thoroughly searched. As I carried a letter from the British Consul, however, I was driven by car to Gibraltar. There I saw, for the first time, a Scotsman wearing a kilt. I waited for a few days in a hotel and one night was taken on board a troopship to share a cabin with three Englishwomen who had survived the siege of Malta, but whose nerves had been wrecked by the experience. To my great surprise each had a bottle of whisky with her. They told me that Malta suffered heavily from air attacks during its long ordeal. It had 3,343 alerts. By the end of 1941 over 14,000 tons of bombs had fallen on 112 square miles of Malta and the small island of Gozo. The enemy lost over 1,000 aircraft, and in the island's defence 58 British aircraft were lost. Civilians killed or died of injuries numbered 1,486. More casualties would have been inflicted if a large proportion of the people had not slept in the rock caves. (After the war King George VI awarded the George Cross to the island for its bravery.) We went in convoy with nineteen other ships. The troops were sleeping on different decks and there were many hundreds of Poles who had been deported from the Soviet Union in 1939 and had made their way to the Middle East via Iran, whilst others had escaped through France from the prison camp Miranda. I heard for the first time from them about the massacre at Katyn. Later, I was to hear that I had lost my brother-in-law there – he had been murdered with 12,000 other Polish officers. Some of the Poles on board were ill and needed to be given some strength and so I managed to procure a bottle of wine. We were on board for Easter and I remember attending Mass which was celebrated by a Scots chaplain. He and the British troops were overjoyed to hear the Poles singing hymns loudly and with such fervour.

The route which the convoy followed was a long one and we sailed almost to the mid-Atlantic. Once the German U-boats and an aircraft tried to attack us and the ship had a near miss. We had constant boat drills. It took eight days from Gibraltar to reach Bristol.

At Bristol we docked on 1st May. All the troops disembarked and I was left alone until finally a policewoman came and took me on a train to London where, to my surprise, I was interned for two days. (Ryder, op.cit. pp.99-115)

Telegrams in the archive of the Polish Underground Movement Study Trust, dated 12 and 14 December 1942, indicate that the Polish Intelligence Service in London had asked for an all-out effort to be made to send Zofia to Spain. (Email with Heide Pirwitz, 27 May 2014) One imagines the British intelligence officers in Spain and Gibraltar had informed London of her imminent arrival.

Like all refugees arriving in Britain during the war, she was taken to London for questioning. Women refugees at this time were interrogated in offices on Nightingale Lane in Clapham by specialist intelligence officers, partly to determine whether she was an enemy agent but also to obtain as much information from her about the military, economic and political situation behind enemy lines as well as details of the assistance she was given in getting to England. Some refugees were then identified as potential recruits to be sent back to their countries as secret agents.

The Secret Intelligence Service (SIS) collated the data and passed it on to relevant departments. Within SIS was rooms where I slept deeply on a mattress.

We could not remain in this village and I asked the teacher to find a mountaineer who could make arrangements to board a train to Barcelona and report to the British Consul there. I was in a dilemma and although it was strictly forbidden to ask someone else to report to the Consul and use the password "I am a member of the Chisholm Clan", I did so. On the man's arrival at the Consulate however the receptionist and guard sent him away. He returned to us in an angry mood. The poor teacher could only advise us to take a bus ourselves from the next village, which was bigger, and he produced money for the tickets.

At 4 a.m. as the bus approached, policemen, unfortunately came to inspect the passengers' papers. It was therefore impossible to proceed and we had to walk. After a mile or two, two engineers in a car gave us a lift for a very short distance. Again, the police stopped the vehicle to check the papers, as we were still near the frontier. We succeeded in getting out of the back seat and hid in a ditch. Either the police failed to see us or we were lucky and the engineers were important people – I will never know the answer – and we continued our long, long walk – 60 kilometres the first day in hot sunshine. We had had nothing to eat or drink. We saw a young girl with two slices of bread and two little salty fishes. We begged her to give these to us. I gave my fish to Gilbert, who then suffered from a frightful thirst and we had to stop and lick water from half-melted icicles.

On our way we passed through part of Catalonia where during the Spanish Civil War (1936 – 1939) many bridges and villages had been destroyed and lay in ruins. Some were still uninhabited, but for safety we kept to the higher part of the mountains. The Spanish police had orders to hand over to the Gestapo anyone escaping.

In the darkness, just before midnight, we found an empty house and were able to lie down in the hay. When we woke in the early light we found ourselves on the edge of a precipice and might easily have turned over and rolled down to our deaths.

As we approached Manresa we met a young boy and asked him to buy us our tickets with the money the teacher had given us. I had not been conscious of days passing, but someone reminded me it was 1st April, and at 6 a.m. we caught the train to Barcelona. Gilbert reported to the French Consulate with the hope of joining the Free Forces. We promised to meet at the Poste Restaurant in Toulouse after the war, but sadly I never heard from him again.

As the British Consul did not arrive before 10 a.m., I waited inside the house and admired its beauty. There was a Spanish maid on her knees washing the floor. I was absolutely filthy. The Consul had already received a telegram from London asking where Zo was. He was advised of my identity and my *other* name of Zofia Zofkowska [sic], No. 30030, and my password which was "I am a member of the Chisholm Clan."

After I had met the Consul and had been fitted out with clothing, I went down to the pier and there to my astonishment was one of the Polish couriers, Lipkowski. Despite his arrest at Figueras he had managed to destroy the post and messages he carried. He advised me to wait as he believed we could reach Lisbon and from there might get a lift on an aircraft to London, but I thought this waiting period might take too long.

A few days later I begged the Consul to get me away as soon as possible, and I boarded a train for Madrid. There the Polish Consul took me to a very a section known as MI9. It funded and supported the escape lines which helped refugees, downed air crews, escaped prisoners-of-war and other personnel escape from occupied Europe. They would have been particularly interested in Elzbieta's escape route and the identities of those who helped her.

Another top secret organisation, the Special Operations Executive (SOE), was set up in July 1940, had been tasked with selecting and training agents to be infiltrated behind enemy lines on special missions as well as dropping supplies to the various resistance movements. They recruited both men and women from amongst these refugees who were will to return to their countries on secret missions.

The SOE officer responsible for Poland, Czechoslovakia and Hungary was Lieutenant Colonel Harold Perkins, code-named MP. The head of the Polish Section was Major Mike Pickles (MPP). Its Operations Officer was Captain R.G Colt-Williams (MPC); its Training Officer was Captain C.T. Gregor (MPG) and its Intelligence Officer was Captain L.M. Massey (MPX1). One imagines they were aware of Elzbieta''s visit as they had to arrange her flight back to Poland. (Walker, J. (2011), *Poland Alone: Britain, SOE and the Collapse of the Polish Resistance 1944*, History Press)

According to her personnel file in the National Archives in Kew, she was brought by the HMS *Stirling Castle* to Liverpool, not Bristol. Her eldest brother, Alfons, she reported, was a regular army officer who had died in 1936. Egon, the next eldest, was also a regular army officer but in the spring of 1942 the German authorities informed his parents that he had died in a concentration camp. Klara, Elzbieta's 20-year-old younger sister, was imprisoned in Myslowice. (TNA HS9/1635/3)

Her personnel file included reports on her interrogation at Nightingale Lane. However, the name on her file was not Elzbieta Zawacka. There were two, Zofia Zajkowska and Elizabeth Watson, the English name she was given by the

British Consul in Spain. In her interview with Anna Muller, she admitted liking the name Elizabeth, using the aliases of Elizabeth von Brauneg and Elizabeth Kubitza. 'I knew my legend (cover story) so well, it grew on me so strongly that I ceased to be Elzbieta Zawacka. I had been a liaison (courier) since the beginning of the conspiracy. I knew how to behave. I knew various tricks indispensible while crossing the border illegally.' (Muller, op.cit. p.120)

Given her three years of experience in courier work, it is interesting to note what information she chose to tell her British interrogators.

Miss ZAJKOWSKA concluded her Secondary Schooling and matriculated in Torun in 1927. She then attended the University of Poznan and obtained her Degree in Mathematics there, after which she obtained a post as Schoolteacher in the German minority school at Sompolono near Lodz, where she worked until 1934.

In 1934 Miss ZAJKOWSKA was transferred to the Girls Secondary School of the "Urszulanki Sisters" at Otorowo near Szamotouly where she worked for one year and was then transferred to the State Secondary School at Poznan. In 1936 she was attached to the Girls Secondary School at Tarnowski in Upper Silesia.

In 1937 on instructions received from the Polish Military authorities, D.O.K. 5 (Col. GIZA – now in the U.K.), Miss ZAJKOWSKA gave up her teaching and was appointed Commanding Officer to the "Przyzposobieni Wojskow Kobiet" (Women's Army Corps) for Upper Silesia. She remained at this post until the outbreak of war.

On the 3.9.39 Miss KAJKOWSKA and her instructors, withdrew from Upper Silesia with the Polish Forces and by way of Lublin reached Lwow [Lviv]. There

Photographs of Elzbieta as a young woman (Top: http://
niepoprawni.pl/blog/1948/elzbieta-zawacka-drzeli-przed-nia-koledzy
-z-podziemia Bottom: http://www.cowtoruniu.pl/artykul-2521)

Elzbieta Zawacka

Photographs of Elzbieta as a young woman: (Top: http://
niezlomni.com/?p=6200 Bottom: http://upload.wikimedia.org/
wikipedia/en/2/2e/E.Zawadzka_Zo_1943.png)

Photographs of Elzbieta as an older woman. Top: http://dzieje.pl/
aktualnosci/gen-elzbieta-zawacka-kurierka-ak-patronka-mostu-
przez-wisle; Bottom: http://nowahistoria.interia.pl/polska-
walczaca/news-elzbieta-zawacka-jedyna-kobieta-wsrod-
cichociemnych,nId,1059279

Elzbieta Zawacka

Photographs of Elzbieta as an older woman. Top: http://
www.cowtoruniu.pl/artykul-2521 Bottom: Polish Underground
Movement (1939-1945) Study Trust, London)

Stefan Grot-Kowecki, Commander of the Home Army in Poland ,who gave Elzbieta the mission to carry intelligence to London. (http://wyorcza.pl/1,76842,7311273,Stasi_i_ general_Grot_Rowecki.html)

Women members of the Home Army in Warsaw, in which Elzbieta was a captain. (http://www.biega.com/brave-women.shtml)

Elzbieta Zawacka

Walker, J. (2011), Poland Alone: Britain, SOE and the Collapse of the
Polish   Resistance 1944, History Press

Walker, J. (2011), Poland Alone: Britain, SOE and the Collapse of the Polish
Resistance 1944, History Press

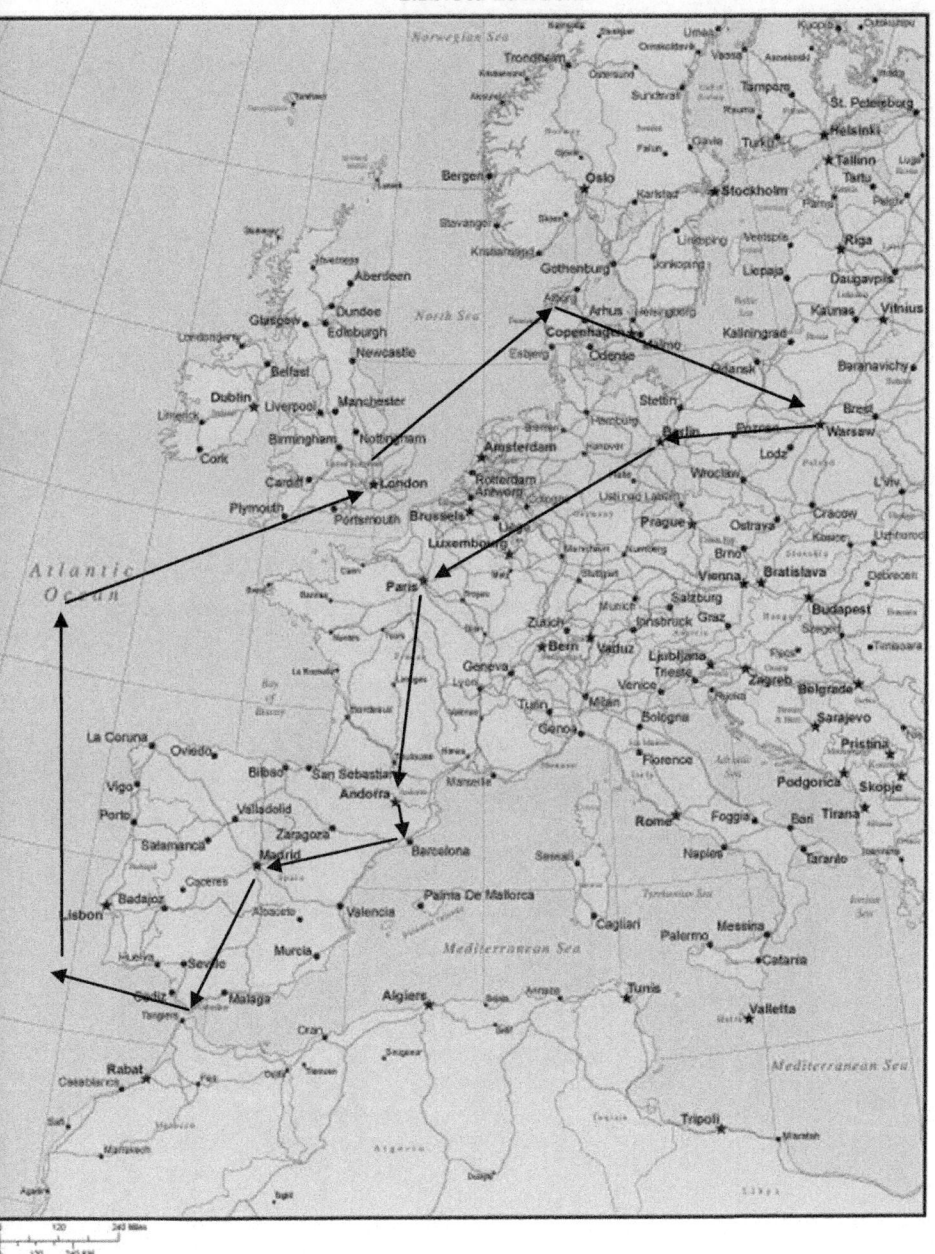

Elzbieta's round trip November 1943—September 1943

Kazimierz Leski in 1941. Code-named Bradl, he was the organiser of Zadroba's escape routes through France. (http://www.rp.pl/artykul/348628.html)

The Kommandtur (German Headquarters), 1 Place d'Opera, Paris , where Elzbieta had to register on arrival and obtain ration cards and an accommodation permit. (http://www.ww2incolor.com/rating/3.5?g2_itemId=362227)

Elzbieta Zawacka

Hotel Deux Mondes, where Elzbieta stayed first in Paris, but, with too many Gestapo officers, she moved. (www.delcampe.net)

Hotel Etats Unis, where Elzbieta also stayed in Paris, but the presence of inquisitive German women encouraged her to move. (www.hoteletatsunis opera.com)

Hotel Voltaire, on the West Bank in Paris, where Elzbieta moved
into safer accommodation. (www.terresdecrivains.com)

Hotel Franklin, the last hotel in Paris where Elzbieta stayed. (http://
www.tripadvisor.co.uk/LocationPhotoDirectLink-g187147-d261990-
i84553191-Hotel_Franklin_D_Roosevelt-Paris_Ile_de_France.html)

HMS Stirling Castle, the ship that brought Elzbieta from Gibraltar to England in May 1943. (www.shipsnostalgia.com)

Nightingale Lane, Balham, where Elzbieta and other women refugees were interrogated by British Security officers on arriving in Britain. (http://www.nightingalehammerson.org/uploads/tx_banner/nh-house_01.jpg)

Elizabeth Watson, as Elzbieta was known in Britain in 1943. (Ryder, S. (1986), *Child of my Love*, Collins Harvill)

Sue Ryder (later Baroness Ryder of Warsaw), member of the FANY who looked after the Polish agents at various requisitioned country houses in Britain and drove them, including Elzbieta, to RAF Tempsford for her flight (http://www.dsh.waw.pl/pl/4_1068)

Rubens Hotel, 39 Buckingham Palace Road, London, where the Polish General Staff was based during the war. (http:// www.panoramio.com/photo/75406906)

Meeting of the Polish Government-in-exile in London. Elzbieta was reported as meeting President Wladyslaw Raczkiewicz and Generals Wladyslaw Sikorski, Kazimierz Sosnkowski and Joseph Haller. (http://collections.yadvashem.org/photosarchive/en-us/29206.html

General Wladyslaw Sikorski, Prime Minister of the Polish government-in-exile and Commander-in-Chief of the Polish Armed Forces. Died in a plane crash near Gibraltar in July 1943. (http://en.wikipedia.org/wiki/W%C5%82adys%C5%82aw_Sikorski)

Wladyslaw Raczkiewicz, President of the Polish government-in-exile. (http://en.wikipedia.org/wiki/W%C5%82adys%C5%82aw_Raczkiewicz#mediaviewer/File:Raczkiewicz_W.jpg)

Elzbieta Zawacka

General Kazimierz Sosnkowski succeeded Sikorski as General
Inspector of the Polish Armed Forces. (http://en.wikipedia.org/wiki/
Kazimierz_Sosnkowski)

Jan Jankowski, delegate to the Polish Government-in-exile, who was
present during one of Elzbieta's interviews in London. (http://
commons.wikimedia.com/JanStanislawJankowski)

Bernard O'Connor

SOE's HQ from 1940 to 1945 was in rooms above Marks and Spencer's office, 64 Baker Street London. Known officially as the "Inter -Services Research Bureau" but to others as "the firm", "the racket" or "the outfit". (http://www.culture24.org.uk/places+to+go/london/tra14553)

Major Harold Perkins, SOE's head of Poland, Czechoslovakia and Hungary. (http://www.specialforcesroh.com/gallery.php? do=view_image&id=14657&gal=gallery)

Briggens, near Roydon, Essex, where Poles were stationed until 1942. (http://www.derelictplaces.co.uk/main/ showthread.php?p=231584#post231584)

Audley End, near Saffron Walden, Hertfordshire was used by the Poles for paramilitary training from 1942. Elzbieta stayed here before her flight back to Poland.
(http://www.english-heritage.org.uk/daysout/properties/audley-end-house-and-gardens/#Right)

Ringway aerodrome, now Manchester Airport, where Poles, including Elzbieta were given parachute training.

Daytime parachute drop into the grounds of Tatton Park, adjacent to Ringway Aerodrome. Elzbieta would have had up to three drops from an air balloon and two from a Whitley bomber, including a night drop.
(http://www.army.cz/images/id_7001_ 8000/7419/assassination-en.pdf)

Tatton Park, adjacent to Ringway, where Elzbieta and other agents were accommodated during their parachute training. (personalpages.manchester.ac.uk/staff/harold.somers/coling/tattonpark.jpg)

Postcard of Arisaig, inverness-shire, Northwest Scotland, where SOE provided paramilitary training. Although undocumented, Elzbieta may have undergone four-to-five weeks of training with other women agents.

Still from 1944 film. Now the Story can be Told'. Sue Ryder drove Elzbieta and two other Polish agents to RAF Tempsford for their flight. (Still from 'Now the Story can be Told, The Imperial War Museum)

Still from 1944 film 'Now the Story can be Told showing agents being escorted into Gibraltar Farm for a final briefing before their flight. (The Imperial War Museum)

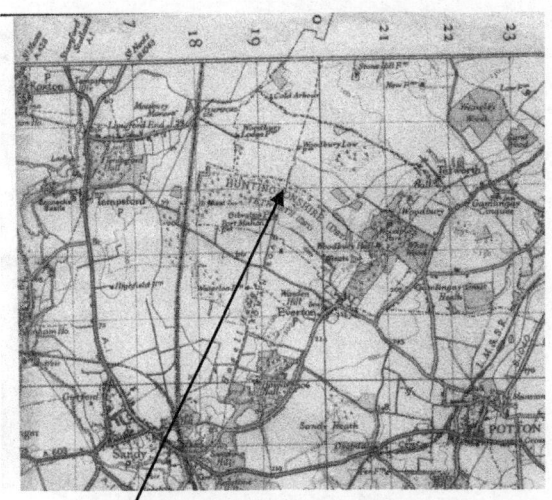

1930s map showing location of RAF Tempsford, about fifty miles north of London, where Elzbieta flew from in September 1943.

Inside Gibraltar Barn where agents were kitted out prior to their flight. Today it is a memorial to all the brave men and women flown out between 1942 and 1945 by 138 and 161 Special Duties Squadrons (including the Polish C Flight).

Photographs of Elzbieta in later years. Top: http://i.ytimg.com/vi/
rlp9sj87eWQ/0.jpg Bottom: http://kohr.kujawsko-pomorskie.pl/
Profesor-Elzbieta-Zawacka/Pani-Profesor-i-Jej-Fundacja

Elzbieta Zawacka

Photographs of Elzbieta in later years. Top: http://www.um.torun.pl/
torun/baza/pierwsza.php?status=0&news_id=7356 Bottom: http://
www.um.torun.pl/torun/baza/pierwsza.php?
status=0&news_id=7356

she was attached to the Women's Battalions, with which she remained until the surrender of Lwow on the 22.9.39. After the occupation of the town by Russian troops Miss ZAJKOWSKA worked with the Women's Battalions in their underground activities.

On orders received from the Z.W.Z. (Polish Army "Underground" Organisation), Miss ZAJKOWSKA left Lwow, travelling by train to Sanck, where she crossed the Russian/German demarcation line and reached Katowice. Shortly afterwards she left for Warsaw.

After reporting to the Z.W.Z. Headquarters, she was sworn in and remained in Warsaw undergoing special training. Afterwards she returned to Upper Silesia where, until January 1941, she was in charge of the secret organisation of the Women's Armed Forces.

In January 1941 Miss ZAJKOWSKA was recalled to Warsaw and until her departure to this country worked as a courier between Warsaw, Poznan and Berlin. Speaking German fluently and being issued with a forged Volksdeutsch, brown Identity card, she never encountered any difficulties in performing her duties.

She claims that of the three different routes between Warsaw and Berlin, Kutno was the most difficult one and the control [check point] very strict; the control at Poraj was also very strict at times, but the easiest control point was Trzebinia.

In December 1942 Miss ZAJKOWSKA was informed that she would be sent to London with a special message to the Polish Military Authorities. She was issued with a forged Identity Card of the type issued to German officials and leaving Warsaw by train on the 17.12.42 she took the route through Berlin, Leipzig, Frankfurt and Saarbrucken to Paris. The journey was uneventful and after arrival in Paris she reported to the Z.W.Z. authorities.

There, however, she was informed that owing to the arrests on the French/Spanish border and to the heavy snow-falls in the Pyrenées, she would have to wait until her journey was safely arranged. She waited until the 28.1.43 when realising that her instructions were getting out of date she returned to Warsaw for new instructions.

She left Warsaw again on the 9.2.43 and reached Paris by the same route. She claims that on both occasions there was a strict control on the train between Leipzig and Berlin; on this sector everyone's papers were inspected three times. The next closely controlled part of the journey was through Alsace, where all documents were seen both by the Military Police and Kriminalpolizei in mufti [plain clothes]. (TNA HS9/1635/3)

Additional details of this journey were found in the transcript of an interview she had in London on 10 May 1943.with Jan Jankowski present. He was a delegate of the Polish government-in-exile who became deputy Prime Minister in 1944.

Journey.

Miss Watson left WARSAW on 9 February, 1943. She had papers establishing her identity as a Volksdeutsche [German term of ethnic Germans living outside the Reich]. She speaks perfect German, and asked in that language for a ticket to PARIS at the railway station. No questions were asked, nor was she required to produce any identity papers, but she was given a ticket only as far as SAARBRUCKEN, as for technical reasons a through ticket could not be issued. The ticket (second class express train) cost 170 Zls. [Zlotys, Polish currency]

The train on which she travelled was for Germans only, and it only took her as far as the

Friedrichstrassebahnhof in BERLIN. Her papers were examined once at KUTNO (frontier station between the General Government and the Reich). She stayed the night at BERLIN and left the following day from the Anhalterbahnhof to Saarbrucken via Leipzig. The papers of all passengers in this train were checked on three occasions by Kripo [Kriminalpolitzei, the German equivalent to the CID] men.

Papers carried.

She had the following papers, supplied by her organisation in WARSAW.

Kennkarte, showing she was a Volksdeutsche from Warsaw. She had other similar Kennkarte [identity card] previously, and they had always passed muster.

A certificate of employment with the Rustungkommando, Warsaw, bearing a photograph. This paper was similar in form to the Kennkarte.

A certificate from the same office to the effect that she was travelling on official business, Paris, and calling upon all German authorities to expedite her journey.

A green Durchlessschein. [travel permit]

A Devisenschein [currency exchange certificate] authorising her to take out the equivalent of 600 Zls. in German or French currency.

Forged Reisemarken. [German currency]

General Impressions of Germany.

The food situation is much worse than in England, the people are fairly well dressed, although not as well as here. Considerable despondency was evident and in general morale appeared to be fairly low.

Conditions in Poland.

Railways. These are controlled by Germans, and a fair proportion of the lower personnel is also German (about 50%) (TNA HS9/1635/3)

In a memo dated 10 May 1943, Major H. J. Baxter wrote to Captain N. G. Nott, both Intelligence officers, expressing concern that,

> She had been released too quickly for Stokes [the interviewing officer at Nightingale Lane] to question her further about conditions in Poland and it was hoped that she would pay them a visit or answer a questionnaire. . 'She is in a position to give us a vast amount of information about every type of matter which is of interest in checking stories of Poles coming from that country... There is one other point which arose during the course of the case; Stokes became aware that neither of the names used by this woman was actually her real name. The alien did not give to Stokes her proper name and this has been recorded in my file in a sealed envelope. This seems to add unnecessarily to the mystery of the case, and I should be glad to know from you if you think there is any reason why this name should continue to be recorded in this sealed envelope or whether it can be placed openly on the file which is, in any event, a Y. Box file. [One imagines the name was Elzbieta Zawacka.] (TNA HS9/1635/3)

Another memo, dated 1 June 1943, from D/CE/LI (?) to D/CE/SS (Dicky Warden), officers in SOE's Security Section, revealed that,

> MP [Perkins] rang up yesterday to say he approved circulation of the attached report in this form, within the organisation but he was rather reluctant to have it passed to 'C' [Code-name of the Secret Intelligence Service (SIS)], as the lady in question has arrived in this country entirely unknown to the Polish Deuxieme Bureau [Intelligence Service], and he wishes to keep this arrival secret from them at all costs. He suggests, if you agree,

that A/CD [Air Commodore Archibald Boyle, Director of SOE's Intelligence Section] should decide whether the report is to go to 'C', and if it is sent, an absolutely explicit undertaking should be obtained from 'C' that the report does not reach the Poles, nor is the arrival of the lady mentioned to them in any form. (TNA HS9/1635/3)

Perkins' comment after he had met Elzbieta was that, 'This straight-forward, intelligent and very brave woman has undoubtedly contributed greatly to the common effort and I feel that there should be some recognition for her services." (Quoted in Maresch, op.cit.p.14) There is no evidence that she received any British commendation.

The questionnaire that she was asked to complete and her responses provided fascinating details about conditions in Poland and Germany and her journey to Britain.

TRAVEL
TICKETS
Are there any formalities over buying a railway ticket in the general Government? No
(B) If so, how they affect –
.Germans? None
Volkdeutsche? None
Poles?
Permission to leave WARSAW is required, and may be obtained at the station a few hours before departure. (There is a black market in such passes at the WARSAW railway station.) The passes are issued at a special window and look like railway tickets. They are issued on the strength of a certificate from a firm that the journey is a business one.
Similar regulations apply to other stations, e.g. KRAKOW, OSROWIEC, SKARZYSKO
For journeys –

inside the General Government? As above.
Over the General Government frontiers?
There are certain express trains, e.g. WARSAW-
POZNAN-BERLIN, WARSAW-KATOWICE-
VIENNE, which are for Germans only. Certain
express trains do not take German civilians and
this is indicated on the timetables.

Would an obvious foreigner have any difficulty over buying a
railway ticket in the General Government? Not answered.

Are documents ever called for when buying a ticket?

(a) to a destination inside the General Government? No.

(b) to a destination outside the General Government?

e.g. (i) Germany?

    (ii) Western European Countries?

In buying a ticket to SOSNOWIEC or KATOWIEC, E.W. had
to produce a Durchlassschein, but when she bought a
ticket at the railway station to SAARBRUCKEN no papers
were asked for. J bought a ticket at the Mitropa travel
office in WARSAW and PARIS without being required to
produce documents.

Where are the frontier controls on the lines –
Berlin-Brussels-Paris? Not known,
Berlin-Saarbrucken-Metz-Paris? Several between
    SAARBRUCKEN and METZ, during travel and at
    stations.
Berlin-Strasbourg-Metz-Paris? Not known.

2. TRAINS

Are there any restrictions affecting the right of a ticket-holder
to board a train in the General Government?

Poles are not allowed to travel in trains or compartments
marked "Nur fűr Deutsche", otherwise there are no
restrictions affecting the right of a ticket holder to board a
train in the General Government.

Are there "snap" document inspections on trains inside the
General Government, or are there only ticket inspections?

None, except in the case of a general search. Control of
documents takes place occasionally in sleeping

compartments for Poles on the WARSAW-KRAKOW line.

Are Poles or Volksdeutsche allowed to travel by special trains, or in 1st or 2nd class compartments?

Volkdeutsche travel on all trains except those which are marked in the time tables as reserved for troops only. There is a second class compartment for Poles in the WARSAW-KRAKOW train.

3. FRONTIERS

Can a ticket be bought to a point across the General Government frontiers without formality? If not, what are the formalities?

See 1.(D) (b).

How are the document controls carried out at –

(i) Kutno?

(ii) Poraj?

Trzebinia?

The Durchlassschein and the Marschbefehl [Soldier's marching orders], or an equivalent paper are checked at all frontier points; the identity card is not always checked; the Devisenschein [financial exchange certificate] is most strictly checked at KUTNO and least so at TRZEBINIA.

Is it possible easily to avoid them?

If not, how is it easiest to cross out of or into the General Government?

In the control of local frontier traffic of passengers in slow trains all passengers have to leave the train and undergo control at the Zollamt at PORAJ. The same applied in 1941 to ZYCHLIN near KUTNO but it is believed that it no longer applies to this frontier point. Evasion of control is very difficult. There are fairly numerous patrols all around the train. However, a case is known in which an overcrowded express train from WARSAW-POSNAN, travelling during the holiday season, was not controlled at all. It is always possible to cross the frontier illegally, at unauthorised points.

Illegal traffic across the frontier is very brisk, and consists both of smugglers and of others. The frontier is closely patrolled by the Grenzpolizei [German border police].

Is there to your knowledge much unauthorised travel in and out of the General Government?

What steps, if any, do the General Authorities take to stop this?

Do you know anything about the Passtelle in Warsaw or Cracow?

Do you know anything about travel documents issued to Poles or Foreigners employed in the following institutions?

Todtorganisation?

Heeneskraftfahrpark?

Bauleatung der Luftwaffe?

The Foreign Army Supply Column Drivers (S.I.M.C.O.)? Not known.

4. DOCUMENT CONTROLS

(A) In your experience where are the chief document control points, other than frontiers between –

(i)   Warsaw-Berlin?

(ii)   Berlin-Paris?

Warsaw-Vienna?

Warsaw-Baltic Ports?

Berlin-Baltic Ports?

Berlin-North Sea Ports?

Berlin-Rhineland?

Knows only of snap controls of documents by the Kripo and Gendarmerie on the lines WARSAW-BERLIN, KATOWICE-BERLIN, and BERLIN-FRANKFURT a/M.

Have you encountered any controls near Hanover on the Berlin-Brussels line? Not known.

5. MISCELLANEOUS

(A) How did you arrange to draw rations?

In restaurants and in restaurant cars using forged Reisenmarken received from the Organisation [Polish Home Army].

(B) Have you had any dealings with the Reiselbensmittelausgabebiuro [sic]? No.

(C) What would the easiest way to draw rations on a journey from Warsaw to Paris for a person travelling on unauthorised documents?

Rations should be taken with one. Restaurants, including those at railway stations, supply Stammgericht, coffee and beer without ration cards. Food cannot be obtained in restaurant cars without rations unless the waiter is squared before meal time.

(D) Have you any knowledge of the Workers Hostels (for workers travelling to and from work in Germany) such as the one at Aachen?

(E) Have you any knowledge of the Auslands-versammmburgsstelle isic] n Berlin? Do you know any travellers who have been detained there?

(F) What formalities did you have to comply with in hotels in –

(i) Berlin? Fill in the Meldekarte [Registration card], giving the number of identity card and of the frontier pass.

(ii) Paris? She had to submit a Quartierschein [Accommodation form] issued her by the Kommandantur [German headquarters]. In French hotels E.W. and J. [?] filled in "Fiches". In certain cases the hotel management demanded identity papers for the purpose of checking.

6.GERMAN BILLETS

Source has been billeted by the German Kommandantur in a Hotel in Paris. Can she state in which hotels in Paris are the Germans being billeted by the Kommandantur Wehrmacht?

Gestapo?

Other officials?

There are many Gestapo officers in the Hotel Deux Mondes on the Avenue de l'Opera, PARIS.

The Hotel des Etats Unis on a side street off the Avenue de l'Opera houses chiefly civilian officials, including a large number of women. The Hotel Voltaire on the Quai Voltaire is occupied by German civilians. A large number of German troops are in the Hotel Franklin near the Cadet Metro Station.

Any German may ask to see a list of hotels requisitioned for Germans, as well as a list of restaurants etc. for Germans kept at the Kommandantur. (TNA HS9/1635/3)

Further details of her Interrogation with Major Geoffrey Wethered, one of the Security officers, were included in another report, dated 20 May 1943. On this occasion she was referred to by her English name of Elizabeth Watson.

<u>Travelling between Warsaw and Berlin.</u>

Miss Watson says she has lived in Warsaw ever since her return there at the beginning of 1941, except of course, for her various journeys to Berlin and about Poland.

She cannot remember the exact number of her journeys from Warsaw to Berlin, but thinks she must have made this journey six or seven times. She generally travelled through Silesia, via Cracow or via Poraj and Trzebinia. The strictest control is at Kutno, where people are thoroughly searched. She came this way on her last journey. Although she usually travelled with a Volksdeutsch identity card, on two occasions she stopped with friends in Silesia who gave her Reichsdeutsch papers with which to continue her journey to Berlin. The Reichsdeutsch identity card is grey in colour and folded in two. On her final journey she travelled right through to Paris with her brown Volksdeutsch card issued in Warsaw.

She was never controlled on the trains in 1941, but during her journey to France she met with frequent controls. She is sure she was never recognised by any of the officials on the trains. For one thing, the trains were always very full and besides, she never bought a through ticket to Berlin, nor travelled right through on the same day. She always broke her journey at some intermediate station and took another ticket. She sometimes stopped a couple of days in Breslau. She always got her ticket at a station, except on one occasion when she bought an extension to her ticket to a station beyond her original booking. She was never asked for her papers or controlled in any way when buying a ticket at a station.

In 1941 the only controls were by the frontier guards, but since 1942 there have also been Police controls, but no frequent demands to see papers. The crossing of the border between German and Polish territory in Poland is not very difficult. She says she must have crossed this border from 100 to 150 times in the course of her travelling and has never had any trouble. She sometimes crossed on foot and sometimes by train and generally there was no control at all. She only ever used her Reichsdeutch card on the Silesian side of the frontier and the Volksdeutsch one on the Polish side. For travelling within Poland she normally carried an identity document with a fingerprint but no photograph. On her journeys to Berlin she carried the following identity documents:-

Kennkarte (either Volksdeutsch or Reichsdeutsch).
Durchlassschein. Green.

Her Durchlasseschein was always a false one, so she does not know whence these are officially obtained. In fact, all her papers were always forged.

On her journey to Paris in December 1942 she had a Devisenschein authorising her to take 300 Zls. out of the country and in February 1943 a Devisenschein for 600 Zls. The other documents which he carried on her journeys to

Paris were as follows:-
Her Kennkarte (Volksdeutsch).
Ausweiss from the Rustungkommando in Warsaw, showing she was employed by a firm working for them.
A certificate from the named firm stating she was travelling to Paris on business and requesting that facilities be given her on her journey.
At the French frontier the first time, the Gendarmerie were very astonished by this Rustungkommando document, as they had never met its like before. They at first said they ought to telephone to check up on it, but Miss Watson is sure they did not in fact do this.
Her papers on her journeys to Paris entitled her to make a through journey to Paris only. On her return from Paris after the first journey, she did in fact stop a night with some friends in Berlin, as her train was late. She should have reported this to the Police in Berlin, but she did not do so. Had she been asked any questions on her journeys, she would have stuck to her story about working for the firm in Warsaw, but as this firm was non-existent, she would of course have been finished had the authorities ever checked up. Major Wethered asked her if the Germans might have checked up on the firm and on her journeys to Paris with the Rustungkommando since she has been in England. She thinks this is unlikely, because the Paris Kommandantur where she reported at various times is such an enormous department, with so many people passing through, that it could not check up on every individual. She does not think she ever came under suspicion.

Reporting at Kommandantur in Paris.
Immediately on her arrival in Paris she reported her arrival to the Kommandantur. Here there are various counters: At the first there was an Unterofizier and a woman official who dealt with her Meldezettel. To fill this in, she had to give her name, where she had come from

and where she lived, and her reason for coming to Paris. This was signed by the Unteroffizier and one copy was retained by him and the other, a sheet of yellow paper, was given to her. She then went to the second counter to get a Kwartirschein, stated what part of Paris she wanted to live in and was given the name of a hotel. (On the first occasion she was given the Hotel du Monde in the Avenue de l'Opera, which she subsequently found to be full of Gestapo.) she then returned to the first counter where she gave the name of her billeted address to complete the Meldezettel. At the third counter she got her ration card. When acquiring the necessary forms at the Kommandantur, she did not explain her story, but merely handed over all her papers and told the officials they would find all her particulars on them. The men whom she overheard registering were mostly in civilian clothes and stated they were on a special mission.

On her first visit to the Kommandantur, she said she would only be a few days in Paris, but when she discovered that her departure for England was likely to be delayed, she returned to the Kommandantur and said she was going back to Germany for Christmas. In fact she did not do so, but went to stay with some friends in Paris until 28th December, when she again called at the Kommandantur and stated that she had now returned from her Christmas trip to Germany and would be in Paris for some time. In January she made a journey to the South of France, but did not report this to the Kommandantur.

She had two very awkward moments during her stay in Paris:

On her first journey from Warsaw she was issued with forged Reisemarks with which she had no trouble in Paris. On her return in February, however, she was issued in Warsaw with forged Reisemarks of the new 1943 issue. When she presented these at the

Kommandantur in Paris to get her rations, the woman official looked at them very suspiciously as they were too sharply printed. She said they appeared to be forged and that she would check up on them. Miss Watson suggested that she enquire in Warsaw and fortunately the woman changed her mind – in Miss Watson's opinion because of the trouble involved in checking up with Warsaw.

On the second occasion that she reported her arrival in Paris after her professed return to Germany over Christmas – she said she expected to be staying in Paris for some time and was therefore asked to fill in a form giving particulars of her Party Membership. This took her by surprise and she did not know what to fill in, but after studying the form she decided to say she was not a party member.

Another question which she had not been prepared for arose in the course of filling in her Meldezettel the first time. She was suddenly asked the name of the firm in Paris where she was working. She invented the name and address in a street in Montmartre which was at that time the only street she knew. She had not been supplied with an address to give before she left Warsaw and when she returned the next time from Warsaw, she was obliged to give the same false address, as she was using the same cover. Besides, any German travelling to Paris is given a Meldezettel at the Kommandantur on arrival and must keep this and produce it again if he returns to Paris on a second visit. The Meldezettel is also used as an Ausweiss when getting meals in German eating-places in Paris, etc.

She was also asked if she had a Feldpost No., but said she had but [then] said she had none.

She lived in various hotels in the course of her stay in Paris. First the Hotel du [Deux] Monde in the Avenue de l'Opera, later the Hotel des Etats Unis in the same neighbourhood, which proved uncomfortable as it contained some inquisitive German women and after that the Hotel Voltaire on the River Gauche. All this time she was living on German papers, but at the end of her stay, she reported her return to Warsaw to the Kommandantur and was issued with French papers by the Organisation in Paris, showing that she was an Alsatian from Colmar. With these papers she stayed at the French Hotel Franklin.

Paris to Tarascon. She travelled via Vichy, Nimes, Carascon and Toulouse. She left Paris with 3 French officers and they were joined in Vichy by another and by two more at Carascon. The journey was organised in stages and the party had a different guide for each stage. She never knew the correct names of the guides.
The first control of papers was on their entry into the defence area near the Spanish frontier, 3 or 4 kms. from Foix. She was no longer carrying the French papers which she had used in Paris, but papers showing that she had been born in Alsace and was now living in the Pyrenées Orientales. She was convinced that the whole party was done for when they met with this control as all their papers were very badly forged, but they were in fact allowed through. The party was divided up in three compartments; Miss Watson and two others in one carriage, two in another and one in a third. The control was by German frontier Police and was very strict in all the compartments except hers, where they were fortunate in having an old and not very thorough officer to do the control.
Journey over the Spanish Frontier. On arrival in Tarascon, they spent a couple of hours in one hotel, resting and preparing for their journey to the frontier. Late at night they went to another hotel where they were met by the guide. While the whole party was waiting in the hall

of this hotel, all dressed up in their mountain boots and carrying rucksacks, two German soldiers of a mountain regiment, with edelweiss badges on their caps, came in. Miss Watson does not know whether these officers had come to the hotel in order to carry out a control of visitors, or whether they had merely come in for a glass of beer, but at any rate, they asked for the party's papers. All six of them were standing in a row at the back of the hall. While the soldiers were looking at the papers of the first man, Miss Watson, who was at the other end, managed to creep out of the room, by passing behind the rest of the party, into a small room off the hall, where she persuaded the Spanish maid to turn the wireless on very loud. She then left her overcoat and gloves and rucksack in this room and came back into the hall and up the stairs onto the first floor, hoping to be taken for one of the hotel maids if seen by the soldiers. At the top of the stairs, the guide pushed her quickly into a room at the back of the hotel which gave straight out onto the hillside. There she found a group of contrabandiers who were also to cross the frontier with the same guide. They set off over the hill at once, and she later heard that the rest of her party had been taken to Toulouse, whence one of them later managed to escape.

The first night they only went as far as a nearby village, where she spent the night on the house of a Spaniard, a friend or relative of the guide. The guide took fright and left them and next day the party went into the mountains where they remained for three days and two nights and were eventually forced to return to the village. Here she again stayed in the house of the Spaniard and rested for a few days.

Miss Watson then got hold of another guide and set off in a party with some Frenchmen. The party split up and she continued with one French Officer (named Gilbert?) into Andorra. At a little village in Andorra (Canillo?) the

Frenchman saw an Andorran who put Miss Watson in touch with an Englishman named Bertrand, connected with the British Consulate at Barcelona. She told him it was essential for her to reach Barcelona without getting herself into prison. The Englishman said he would provide a good guide – a Spanish "Red" – and he took them as far as Sant Julia in a car. They went on next day from here on foot over the mountains, across the Spanish frontier. At about 8 a.m. they heard the Spanish frontier control and hid themselves. Then the guide unfortunately started to run away, back up the hill, thus attracting the attention of the guard who opened fire. The Frenchman followed the guide and was followed by Miss Watson. She did not manage to get over the hill, but hid in some rocks near the top, from where she could see one of the guards coming towards her carrying a gun. Fortunately, he did not see her and she hid there for about 1½ hours. Then the Frenchman happened to hear her coughing and joined her.

From here they walked in the wrong direction back towards the frontier and spent 3 days in a village (La Bastida) with a schoolmaster, who showed them a map of the route to Barcelona. They were told it would be alright to go by bus to Lerida, but they saw a lot of Police about (in the bus?) and decided to walk. On the road towards Manresa they hailed a passing car containing two Spaniards who gave them a lift. They reached Oliana where they had lunch – Miss Watson and the Frenchman in a cheap restaurant and the Spaniards in a more expensive hotel. They then continued in the car and outside Pons they were stopped by a Spanish patrol of two carabiniers. These looked at the Spaniards' papers, ticked them off for giving lifts to strangers which is forbidden, and said the whole party must go on to a further control. Fortunately, the two members of the patrol decided they would go on in the car, so Miss Watson and the Frenchman were left to follow on foot. They therefore turned off the road into the mountains again. They walked on to Solsona and to Mandresa, mostly along the road, but avoiding towns and villages. They eventually reached Manresa about 4 a.m. and Miss Watson is sure they were not followed. She thinks they took about 48 hours from La Bastida.

She thinks it would be safe for her to return the same route, as the Spanish police think she came via La Figueras. (TNA HS9/1635/3)

Captain Stokes, the interviewing officer at Nightingale Lane, reported what happened next.

20. Near Manresa they entered a small village and there got into touch with a Spanish Schoolteacher. He took care of them and afterwards instructed them on how to reach Barcelona. The next day they went to Manresa and after buying tickets proceeded by train to Barcelona which they reached on the 29.3.43.

21. Miss ZAJKOWSKA reported immediately to the British Consulate and was in their care for six days, after which, she was sent by train to Madrid. There the British authorities issued her with an Emergency Certificate in the name of "Elizabeth WATSON" and ten days after her arrival she left Madrid for Gibraltar, arriving there on 25.4.43. in Gibraltar her Emergency Certificate was taken from her by the Security Officer in the Port.

CONCLUSION.

22. The interrogation of Miss ZAJKOWSKA proved to be rather difficult, as being on a special mission from the underground organisation to the Polish 6eme Bureau in London and having passed through the channels of the organisation practically all the way, she was rather reluctant to pass that information on to me. In order not to make her task more difficult I did not press for details.

23. Miss ZAJKOWSKA seems to be a straight-forward, intelligent and very brave woman. Her sister has been imprisoned by the Gestapo and her parents have been informed that she will be released as soon as Miss ZAJKOWSKA gives herself up to the German authorities. Miss ZAJKOWSKA herself, thinks that the Germans most probably do not know of her activities for the underground organisations but know of her from before the war when she was a Commanding Officer of a Women's Military Movement in Upper Silesia.

24. She is hoping to go back to Poland and for this reason her real name is being kept in a separate envelope at the L.R.C. [London Reception Centre at the Royal Victoria Patriotic School in Wandsworth]

25. After it was confirmed that she was well-known to S.O.E. she was released on the same day after interrogation. (TNA HS9/1635/3)

Part of her mission appears to have been to gain first-hand evidence of the overland escape route so that arrangements could be made for others to use the same method for reaching Britain. A copy of her report is held in the archive of the Polish Underground Movement Study Trust, Piccadilly, London. (Email communication with Heide Pirwitz, 27 May 2014)

In the memoirs she gave to Baroness Ryder, she recalls that after her internment,

>...an English officer appeared who spoke Polish and he escorted me to the Rubens Hotel in Buckingham Palace Road. There, in the foyer, I met Lipkowski again. He had managed to get to London on an aircraft from Lisbon. The last time we had met was in Barcelona. I reported to the Chief of 6 Bureau (the Headquarters for Special Duties. (Ryder, op.cit.p.115)

The Rubens Hotel was where the Polish general staff were based during the war. Research by Ewa and Bogumil Liszewskich for their book, *Brave Women,* included a chapter on Elzbieta Zawacka, which revealed that,

During her stay in Britain, Elzbieta met with key representatives of the Polish civil and military authorities, including President Wladyslaw Raczkiewicz and Generals Wladyslaw Sikorski, Kazimierz Sosnkowski and Joseph Haller. The purpose of the mission was to provide reports on the current situation in the country, agreeing more effective channels of communication with the Polish government-in-exile and to discuss the proposal to recognise the rights of women soldiers serving in the underground army. The result of her mission was, amongst others, a decree by the Polish President on 27 October 1943 for women to be given the status of soldiers in the Polish Army and the right to wear ranks. (Liszewskich, E. & B. (2013), *Brave Women,* Fronde, Warsaw, Translation of chapter: 'Elizabeth Zawacka - the only woman among Cichociemni' appeared on Nowa Historia website, 18 November 2013)

Ryder's research into the Zagroda organisation revealed that it had up to a hundred couriers, half of whom were women. Of the eight that succeeded in reaching London, Elzbieta was the only woman. (Ryder, op.cit.p.120) In her account of her exploits, Elzbieta detailed the intelligence that she passed on.

The information which I, and indeed all couriers, carried covered a multitude of subjects and was intended for the Polish Commander-in-Chief in London, his staff, our own Foreign Office and all relevant ministries. The information concerned:

U-boats in the Baltic
German troop movements
V-1 and V-2 rockets
Auschwitz
Photographs for forged documents
Escape routes
German industry
Munitions factories
Sabotage
Information and plans of enemy aircraft and armour
The Jewish ghettos and the rising in the Warsaw
Ghetto
Co-operation with the Resistance in Hungary and
Germany
Extermination of Poles and Jews, particularly in the
parts annexed by the Reich.

As a courier I was not allowed to know the exact nature
of the information I carried in case I was captured and
subjected to torture.
There, at headquarters, I worked for two months to
discuss and clear up matters concerning my mission.
From headquarters I went to a parachute course at
Ringway near Manchester, and then for further training
in Scotland. I visited several stations of SOE to give
lectures on the work of the Resistance. On one or two
occasions I was allowed by Security to see training
camps for women of the ATS (Auxiliary Transport
Service). (Ryder, op.cit. pp.115-6)

Agents were given parachute training at Ringway
aerodrome (STS 61), now Manchester Airport. FANY (First
Aid Nursing Yeomanry) drivers escorted the agents and
were reported to have done the jumps with them. After
outdoor and indoor practice jumping from different heights,

depending on the weather, everyone was expected to do at least two jumps from a static air balloon and two from a low-flying Whitley bomber. They were fully kitted out in a jump suit, harness, parachute and protective gear and, to make it realistic, one jump had to be at night. During their up to five day stay, most were accommodated at Tatton Park, a requisitioned 19th century stately home adjacent to the aerodrome and the drops were made into the 1,000-acre grounds.

SOE sent most agents to Arisaig, (STS 21) a remote mountainous area of Inverness-shire, North-West Scotland, for their paramilitary training.. It is possible Elzbieta went with a group of other women but no documentation related to this or the visit to Ringway were included in her personnel file. She would have stayed in one of eleven remote hunting lodges which had been requisitioned to accommodate agents. The training, detailed later, would have been the same as the Polish men at Audley End, an early 17th century stately home near Saffron Walden in Essex, about fifty miles north-east of London which had been requisitioned to accommodate and train the 'Cichociemni' (Silent and Unseen), Polish agents destined to be parachuted back into Poland.

As return flights to Poland took at least eight hours,, they were only undertaken during the months of shorter daylight. Consequently, the next available flight were not until September. Given the long wait, another visit was arranged for Elzbieta to see Brigadier Marion Gamwell, the head of the Women's Transport Service, generally known as the FANY. This was the only women's group in the British military that was allowed to carry arms and one imagines she was keen to find out about their organisation and training.

In Eugenia Maresch's "Zo" – General Elzbieta Zawacka, she quoted a letter signed only 'Lieutenant Colonel' (possibly Perkins) to Gamwell.

" am advising you to stress particularly the democratic angle, that it is the people of the country as a whole, who should decide the part which women are to play in this War, rather than the dogmatic ruling of those in power. Elizabeth, as you know, is inclined to take the militant female dictator view of things. (Maresch, op.cit. pp.11)

The outcome of the meeting is unknown but one imagines Elzbieta telling Gamwell about her attempts to ensure that Polish women soldiers had an equal footing with their male counterparts It is worth noting that this was endorsed when the Polish President signed a decree on 27 October 1943. (Maresch, op.cit. pp.11,14-15)

Given Elzbieta's importance in the Polish resistance, SOE was given the responsibility of arranging her return to Poland. As many other Poles had escaped and made their way to England, the SOE accommodated them at Audley End. Between 1942 and 1944, 527 Polish agents were trained at what was known as Station 43. (Valentine, I. (2006), *Station 43: Audley End House and SOE's Polish Section.* Sutton Publishing)

Given her military background, one imagines that Elzbieta would have been particularly interested, especially as the SOE were training increasing numbers of women agents to be infiltrated into enemy-occupied Europe.

In Ian Valentine's *Station 43*, he detailed how clandestine warfare was taught by Major A. Mackus and included physical fitness, map-reading, combat fighting, boxing, kicking, knee blows, wrist and throat holds, knife fighting, silent killing of guards and sentries, rope strangulation and spinal dislocation. The latter were practiced on dummies and live cats. There were also lessons in microdot photography, invisible printing and false identity cards, shooting (pistols, rifles, machine guns, flame-throwers), ammunition storage, driving (motorbikes, cars, trucks, tanks), breaking locks, sabotage and guerrilla warfare, mantraps, mine traps, anti-tank weapons, heavy explosives as well as general espionage, conspiracy and the German language. For practice, there were Lancaster and Halifax bomber fuselages and Valentine tanks in the grounds.

Briefing and despatching were taught by Major Antonio Wejtko and later Colonel Wieronski and lessons included radio communication (Morse, Eureka, Rebecca and S-phones), signals, and night-drops including reception committees.

The final polishing course, which lasted between four and six weeks, included detailed information about rural and urban conditions in the country they were to be sent to; familiarity of enemy bureaucracy, structure, uniforms and equipment of political, military and civil organisations; creating and mastering individual 'legends' (cover stories) and alibis; mock interrogations and resistance to interrogation/torture; checking false documents; safe houses and dead letter boxes; ciphers, codes and invisible inks and examining maps and photographs of their drop zone (DZ) and the location of sabotage targets. (Valentine, Ian (2006), Station 43: Audley End House and SOE's Polish Section. Sutton Publishing, p.43)

A group of FANY officers was based at Audley End to look after the men and, once their training was finished and a flight arranged, drive them to RAF Tempsford. One of them was Sue Ryder, later Baroness Ryder of Warsaw.

Although Elzbieta did not mention Audley End or having met Ryder, in her *Child of my Love,* Ryder stated that Elzbieta was sent there to wait for favourable weather conditions. This would not have been before the time of the first full moon in September. Being the only female agent at the Special Training School, they shared a room.

Prior to her flight, Elyzbieta would have been taken to be kitted out in appropriate Polish clothing for her trip. When refugees arrived in Britain, SOE offered them British clothes in exchange for theirs. Personal belongings were also exchanged, items like hats, gloves, umbrellas, suitcases, soap, perfume and aftershave. The belongings of each nationality were stored in rooms in The Thatched Barn, a large house on the edge of Hatfield. There were fitting rooms below the police station on Savile Row in London and a Jewish tailor and a team of seamstresses were on hand to adjust the clothing as necessary. Elzbieta would have be given authentic Polish clothes, Polish shoes, a Polish suitcase and handbag, soap, perfume and so on. If agents were caught whilst on operations 'in the Field' and found to be wearing anything that came from Britain, it could be a death sentence.

A dentist used to visit Audley End who removed any 'British' fillings and replaced them with Polish ones. Those who chose to, could have a hole drilled into one of their wisdom teeth into which they could insert their 'L' pill. Should they decide to take one, it contained lethal cyanide crystals in a biteable-through thin rubber coating. Some agents hid them in the top inside part of their jacket, in hollowed out wine bottle corks or tubes of lipstick. You would be dead in fifteen seconds if you chewed one. Agents were told that the Catholic Church had given them a special dispensation to use the pill 'in extremis'.

On 9 September, Ryder drove Elzbieta up to RAF Tempsford for her flight. As the passenger windows were blacked out or had curtains drawn, she would have had no idea of the location or the name of the airfield. Ryder would have escorted her and other agents flying out that night into Gibraltar Farm. This was the nerve centre of the operations, where agents would have had a last chance to examine maps and photographs of their DZ and get the most recent weather reports from the meteorological officer.

Given that RAF Tempsford was a secret airfield, the farm had been partially demolished to make it look disused. Roof tiles had been removed, windows broken and doors left unhinged. The runways had grey and green patches painted on them to resemble grass and in places a wide black line was painted across them to look like a hedge continued across them. Other buildings were camouflaged to look like farm buildings. Some were reported to have huge tarpaulins draped over their roofs on which farm building roofs had been painted.

Agents were then taken outside and into an adjoining barn. Despite having typical Bedfordshire weatherboard on the outside, the interior was reinforced with bricks and rows of concrete shelving covered all the walls. There were no doors on the barn, only two heavy curtains to keep the draught out. A stove kept the inside warm. Once inside she would have had to get rid of any British currency, including loose change. This was donated to the RAF Benevolent Fund. Her pockets were emptied and her clothing and even the soles of her shoes were searched to ensure she had nothing on her that would indicate that she had come from Britain. Money was issued, the choice of a revolver or dagger and a selection of pills offered .

As well as the 'L' pill, other 'medications' included 'A' pills for airsickness; blue 'B' pills containing Benzedrine sulphate for use as a stimulant (the amphetamine Mecrodrin was also issued); 'E' pills, a quick-working anaesthetic that would knock a person out in 30 seconds, and 'K' pills, which would induce sleep for up to 24 hours. Some were given 'M & B 693' (May and Baker's sulfapyridine) pills, which were used before penicillin to counter wound infections and reduce the risk of pneumonia and gangrene. There were also 'Q' and 'U' poison pills and halibut liver oil capsules. One deadly poison the SOE issued left no trace except those of endemic syphilis.

For the journey they were given a tin of sandwiches and a flask of coffee with a choice of rum, brandy or whisky. A baggy 'jump suit' was provided to go over her ordinary clothing. Her ordinary shoes would have been stuffed into her pockets and boots with strong ankle supports would have been worn. To give her added chances of surviving the parachute jump, she was given padded supports for her elbows, shoulders and spine, padded gloves and a padded helmet. Some agents were given gold or silver mementos to remember the SOE organisation who had arranged their training and flight. These could be pawned if necessary. The chaplain was there to give them a blessing and often officers from the country section would have been present to wish them farewell.

Elzbieta recalled in her memoirs being flown in a Halifax which took off in the early evening.

> ...we had a long flight ahead of us. Over Denmark the plane was fired on. The route lay over Sweden, from where the plane turned and followed the Vistula river. A small reception committee was waiting for our group of three. I received the signal "Go" from the despatcher and I jumped, followed by my two companions. I was dropped in a small clearing near the woods of Podkowa Lesna, near Warsaw. I did not fall as well as I should have done and slightly hurt my heels, which made it difficult to walk for the next 45 minutes through the woods to spend the remainder of the night in a cottage there. My parachute was buried by members of the underground reception committee – occasionally (and only if it was considered safe) a parachute was smuggled away and made up into articles of clothing. What I wore was subjected to another thorough search, lest any clues of my true identity should betray me in the event of my capture. (Ryder, op.cit. p.116)

In her interview with Anna Muller, she recalled it being 'a wonderful flight' and about the jump she commented, 'I was not approaching the earth but the earth was approaching me. (Muller, op.cit.p.120)

The Liszewskich's research revealed that the two agents who accompanied her on the mission were Boleslaw Polanczyk, code-named 'Crystal', and Frederick Serafinski, code-named 'Ladder'. A reception committee awaited the Halifax near Grodzisk Mazowiecki, a town about 35 kms southwest of Warsaw. As the plane approached, the prearranged Morse signal was flashed with a torch and, once the package and containers were dropped, the three agents jumped.

Taken to Warsaw, Elzbieta continued her courier work. However, the Abwehr, the German counter-intelligence service, had successfully used direction-finding equipment to locate the transmissions of some of the wireless sets being used by the Resistance to transmit and receive coded messages to and from London. As a result, numerous arrests followed and death sentences issued. Zagroda was largely destroyed. (Liszewskich, E. and B., op.cit.)

Between 8 April and 15 July 1944, she escaped arrest by hiding in the convent of the Sisters of the Immaculate Conception at Syzmanow near Sochaczewa and pretending to be one of the novices. The Reverend Mother Sapieha was a close relative of the Cardinal at Krakow and she sheltered Jewish girls and other women wanting to escape the round-ups. (Ryder, op.cit.p.117)

When the Soviet Red Army approached the eastern suburbs of Warsaw, the Polish Home Army started Operation TEMPEST, an uprising against the German forces. Elzbieta came out of hiding, walked to Warsaw and joined one of the Women's Battalions in the Wojskowa Służba Kobiet (WSK), the Women's Army. However, Joseph Stalin, the Soviet President, ordered his troops to halt before entering the city, giving the Germans a chance to retaliate. For just over two months, with no support from the Allies, the Poles fought a losing battle.

Not directly involved with the fighting, she helped care for the wounded, looked after refugees and eventually left the city to continue the fight against the Germans elsewhere. In her account of her work during the Warsaw Rising, Elzbieta detailed how,

After prolonged and bitter fighting the old city fell again into German hands and together with my colleagues we led about seventeen soldiers through the sewers to another part of the capital. For thousands, this was the only way out.

The acute shortages of food, water, medicines and dressings were appalling. I can truthfully say that the only food some of us had was yeast from a brewery which we mixed with drops of water and cooked where and whenever possible.

Later, when I reached Krakow on 4th October 1944, I met an old colleague – a colonel – and offered him one of the used "biscuits". He looked at it and said, "This resembles the Sacred Host."

At the end of September as we were rounded up and marched out I succeeded in escaping and on 2 October 1944 I arrived in Krakow via Czestochowa.

4 October 1944 – February 1945: organiser and courier again – many journeys to Czechoslovakia, Austria, Germany up to the borders of Switzerland and Denmark. (Ryder, op.cit.p.118)

The Liszewskich's report stated that Krakow needed to establish communications with London during which time Elzbieta carried reports, orders and letters detailing the situation in Poland to Germany and Switzerland. For her efforts, Army Command promoted her to captain and then Supreme Command promoted her to major. (Liszewskich, E. & B. op.cit; Maresch, op.cit.p.16) Ryder included Elzbieta's account of one of her missions in January 1945.

The purpose of travelling to Villingen was to leave a

message there for another courier of the Resistance. I was sitting in the carriage of a train while I was carrying documents which indicated that I came from Villingen (Rhine-land). I was returning from a visit to my "husband" who was seriously wounded. I wore mourning and a veil as my "brother" had been killed on the front. One the documents I carried was a false rubber stamp (stempel) plus a signature.

The German police began checking passengers on the train. When they checked the papers of the woman sitting next to me, to my horror I saw that, by a complete coincidence, she had come from the same hospital in Villingen and, of course, her genuine papers bore a completely different rubber stamp and signature. I purposely looked tired, and this shock persuaded me to get some fresh air. I attempted to make my way out of the compartment before the Germans could ask me for my papers. I was interrupted by another policeman, however, who, fortunately, had not seen the right papers on the German woman but, of course, there was always the risk that he might compare them later. (Ryder, op.cit. pp.116-117)

Her last journey, she recalled, was in February 1945 when she heard both the Allied and Soviet guns on the same day. Some of the towns she visited were on fire and she had to take cover under the steps of buildings to avoid being shot.

At the end of the war in 1945, she was demobilised. Her mother had died of skin cancer after spending time in a Gestapo prison. She had lost two brothers, one in Auschwitz, the other in Katyn forest. Unable to accept Soviet occupation, she renewed her contacts with the Polish underground, undertook courier work again in Warsaw and joined the Freedom and Independence Movement, an anti-Communist association. In 1946 she was allocated a job in the State Office of Physical Education and Military Teaching training new recruits but resigned in 1948 and took up teaching again and studied for a doctorate at the University of Lodz.

On 2 September 1951, she was arrested at Olsztyn on suspicion of espionage and sent initially to Mokotow prison in Warsaw and then to prisons in Fordon, Grudziadz and Bojanowo, near Rawicz. All her research was destroyed, making it impossible for her to finish her doctorate. Despite being sentenced to ten years for treason and espionage, she described there being 'a wonderful feeling of unity among us – so many brave men and women.' (Liszewskich, E. & B. op.cit.) Despite claims that she was tortured, she dismissed Muller's questions about prison. 'There is nothing to be proud of. This was not important.' (Muller, op.cit.p.120)

Following an amnesty in February 1955, she was released and eventually found work teaching in Sierpiec and Torun. She started another doctorate in distance learning at the University of Warsaw and worked as a researcher and lecturer at .the universities of Gdansk and Torun. However, the Communist government prevented her from scientific activities and blocked her promotion.

It was not until 1973, when, aged 64, she was made assistant professor and associate professor at the University of Gdansk. She represented Poland, Czechoslovakia and Hungary at the UNESCO International Council for Correspondence Education (ICCE) In autumn 1976 she went on business to London, where he met with representatives of the Polish community. She undertook research in the archive of the Polish Underground Movement Study centre, particularly on the functioning of the General Staff in London during the Second World War. However, the Polish government confiscated the documents she brought back and searched her apartment and university office.

When the Security Service in the Ministry of Internal Affairs closed down her department in 1978, she retired from teaching but remained an active member of the World Union of Home Army Soldiers and cooperated with Solidarity, the Trade Union

Movement.

Six years after the fall of Communism in Poland in 1989, she was appointed Professor of Humanities. Lech Walesa, the Polish President, awarded her the Order of the White Eagle and promoted her to lieutenant colonel. In 1999 she was promoted to a colonel. (Liszewskich, E. & W. op.cit.)

She continued researching the roles of Polish women soldiers and the official opening of the monument to Maria Wittek was the fulfilment of one of Elzbieta's dreams, the official recognition of women soldiers' contribution to Poland's struggle for independence. Wittek was born in 1899 and, from the age of 18, served in the Polish Army and other military organisations in the First and Second World Wars, eventually promoted to Brigadier General in 1991 by Lech Walesa. A life-size bronze statue of her stands in the Warsaw Army Museum.

On 3 May 2006, President Lech Kaczynski promoted Elzbieta to General, only the second woman with that rank in Polish history.

She died on 10 January 2009, one of the most decorated women in Polish history. In recognition of the contribution she made during and after the war, she was awarded the Cross of Valour five times, the Army Medal, the Officer's Cross and later the Commander's Cross with Star of the Order of Polonia Restituta, the Gold Cross of Merit with Swords, the Home Army Cross, the Medal Pro Memoria, the Order of Virtuti Militari, Silver Cross twice. There was a move to persuade the British government to award her the OBE, Order of the British Empire, but, to the disappointment of many Poles, she was only given the British Veterans' Badge. (Maresch, op.cit, p.16; http://en.wikipedia.org/wiki/Elzbieta_Zawacka)

Bibliography
Books and articles

Clark, F. (1999), *Agents by Moonlight*, Tempus

Liszewskich, E. & B. (2013), *Brave Women,* Fronde, Warsaw, Translation of chapter: 'Elizabeth Zawacka - the only woman among Cichociemni' appeared on Nowa Historia website, 18 November 2013)

Maresch, E. *"Zo"* – *General Elzbieta Zawacka*, Rocznkarchwalno-Historycznycaw

Minczykowska, K *Elizabeth Zawacka, "Zelma", "Sulica", "Zo"* (series: Library Foundation Archive Pomeranian AK', t L), Torun 2008, ed. Foundation 'Archives and Museum Pomeranian AK' in Torun

Muller, A. (2009), *Oral History; The Challenges of Dialogue*, Edited by Marta Kurkowska-Budzan and Krysztof Zamorski, John Benjamins Publishing Company

O'Connor, B. (2013), *Churchill's Angels,* Amberley Press

Oliver, D. (2005), *Airborne Espionage: International Special Duties Operations in the World Wars,* The History Press, Stroud

Ryder, S. (1986), *Child of my Love*, Collins Harvill

Valentine, Ian (2006), *Station 43: Audley End House and SOE's Polish Section.* Sutton Publishing

Walker, J. (2011), *Poland Alone: Britain, SOE and the Collapse of the Polish Resistance 1944,* History Press

Websites
http://en.wikipedia.org/wiki/Elzbieta_Zawacka

http:polishgreatness.blogspot.co.uk/2011_12_01_archive.ht ml

http://facet.wp.pl/kat,1034179,wid,14344761,wiadomosc. html?ticaid=112c70

http://www. zawacka.pl/monodram.html

http://nowahistoria.interia.pl/polska-walczaca/news-elzbieta-zawacka-jedyna-kobieta-wsrod-cichociemnych,nld,1059279

Documents in the National Archives, Kew

TNA HS9/1635/3 Zofia Jazkowska/Elizabeth Watson

Bernard O'Connor's publications on or related to RAF Tempsford during World War Two:

RAF Tempsford: Churchill's MOST SECRET Airfield, Amberley Publishing, (2010)
The Women of RAF Tempsford: Heroines of Wartime Resistance, Amberley Publishing, (2011)
Churchill and Stalin's Secret Agents: Operation Pickaxe at RAF Tempsford, Fonthill Media, (2011)
The Tempsford Academy: Churchill and Roosevelt's Secret Airfield, Fonthill Media, (2012)
Agent Rose: The true Story of Eileen Nearne, Britain's Forgotten Wartime Heroine, Amberley Publishing, (2010)
Churchill's Angels: How Britain's Women Secret Agents Changed the Course of the Second World War, Amberley Publishing, (2012)
The Courier: Reminiscences of a Female Secret Agent in Wartime France, (Historical faction) www.lulu.com (2010)
Designer: The True Story of Jacqueline Nearne, www.lulu.com, (2011)
Return to Belgium, www.lulu.com (2012)
Return to Holland, www.lulu.com, (2012)
Bedford Spy School, www.lulu.com (2012)
Old Bedfordians' Secret Operations during World War Two, www.lulu.com (2012)
Henri Déricourt: Triple Agent (edited), www.lulu.com (2012)
Churchill's School for Saboteurs: Brickendonbury, STS 17, Amberley Publishing, (2013)

Churchill's Most Secret Airfield, Amberley Publishing, (2013)
Sabotage in Norway, www.lulu.com (2013)
Sabotage in Denmark, www.lulu.com *(2013)*
Sabotage in Belgium, www.lulu.com (2013)
Sabotage in Holland, www.lulu.com (2013)
Sabotage in France, www.lulu.com (2013)
Blackmail Sabotage, www.lulu.com (2014)
Sabotage in Greece, www/lulu.com (2014)

Purchase books online:
www.lulu.com/spotlight/coprolite

Visit Bernard O'Connor's website:
www.bernardoconnor.org.uk

Elzbieta Zawacka

Printed in Great Britain
by Amazon

45495037R00056